HOME ECONOMICS FOR YOU

GERALDINE HUTCHINSON

BOOK 3

Yourself and Beyond

BLACKIE

Introduction

You are a person or an individual. In some ways you are similar to other people but in other ways you are unique and this means you look different from everybody else and have your own thoughts, characteristics and personality. These unique qualities will show in the way you speak, behave, work, play and even in the way you dress. Home economics helps you to know yourself and develop your own qualities. We have therefore, called the first book in this series, Book 1 – *Yourself*.

Other people in your family and your society are important to you. Those who care for you, those who help you, those who make your leisure time fun, those who share your interests and those you care for. Home economics helps you to learn about and understand other people, their likes and dislikes, their needs and interests. So Book 2 is called – *Yourself and Others*.

Where you live, how you live, the things you have, the things you see, the things you use every day, the world and all the world's resources matter to you. This is your home and your environment and these things affect the way you live and behave. Home economics helps you to learn about the world around you. So Book 3 is called – *Yourself and Beyond*.

Dedication
To the pupils of St. Veronica's School, London SE17.

Illustrations by Jane Cunningham

Contents

First published 1986
ISBN 0 216 91665 8

Blackie & Son Ltd
Bishopbriggs · Glasgow G64 2NZ
Furnival House · 14–16 High Holborn · London WC1V 6BX

Printed in Great Britain by Holmes McDougall Ltd

THE RESOURCES YOU USE — Topic 1

A resource is something that we can use to help us in our lives. Some resources are essential to life, for example food, other resources are helpful, useful and make life easier, such as an electric dish-washer. Therefore some resources are not essential but are useful.

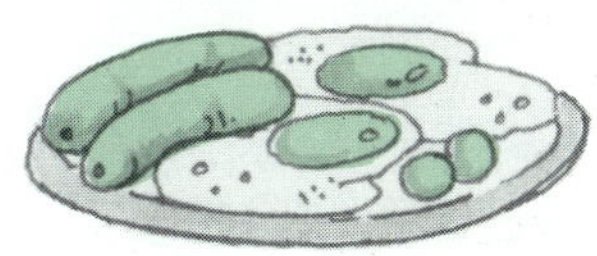

Draw a chart like the one below. On your chart list the names of four resources which you think are essential and write down a reason for your choice. The pictures shown might give you some ideas. An example has been given.

I think these resources are essential	*Reason*
1 Water	
2	
3	
4	

Look at the list of resources below and choose four which you think are *non-essential*. Write a sentence in your book for each of these four resources, explaining why you have chosen it and why you think it is non-essential.

List of resources
Tea maker; refrigerator; oven; kettle; steam iron; radio; newspaper; bracelet; game; car; aftershave; soap; electric tin opener; water; video; dish-washer; camera; make up; toothbrush; computer; grass; trees.

You might like to discuss your answers with your teacher and the rest of the class before you go on.

Through answering the previous questions you will have discovered that there are many different resources.

Water, gas, oil, air, wheat, grass and sea are all resources. These could also be called *natural* resources because they have not been made by man but were already on the earth.

In the margin there are two pictures of natural resources. Draw these pictures in your book and at the side of each one write a sentence to explain how it is used to help in our lives.

Throughout the world natural resources are used. In many cases the natural resources are organized so that more people can reach them or so that they can be used in new places.
For example: drilling for oil and taking it in pipes to new places; piping water to irrigate dry lands; planting seeds to grow lots of wheat which can then be exported to other countries.

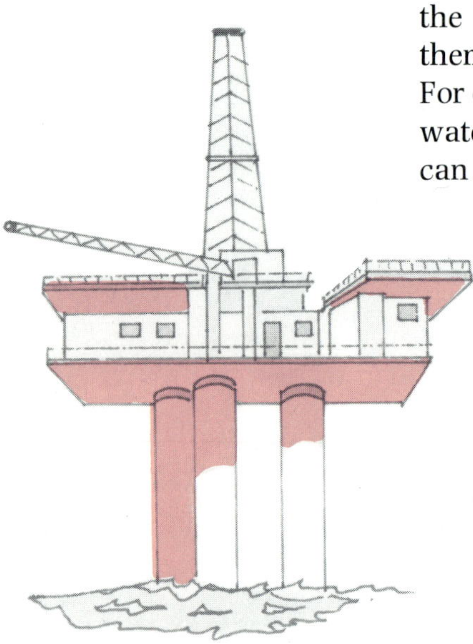

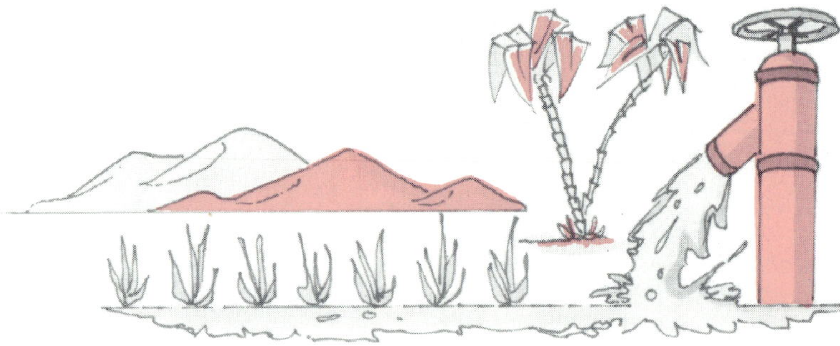

However the supply of natural resources in the world may not be endless and it is important that these resources are used carefully to avoid wastage.

For example, paper is made from wood pulp obtained from trees. So one way of conserving trees is to recycle old paper to make such things as paper bags and envelopes.

Sometimes natural resources like fuel, metals and oil are used to make new resources. We could call these resources *man-made*.
For example: metals are used to make electrical equipment such as, fires, cookers, electric drills, washing machines; oils can be used to make plastics and paint.

Sometimes natural resources are made more interesting or safer, either by adding things to them or by taking things away.
For example: colours or dyes are added to natural fibres such as wool and silk; salt water can be purified and the salt taken away so it becomes drinking water.

Work in twos. Look carefully at the list of resources on page 3. Then draw a chart like the one beside it and decide together which of the resources are natural and which are man-made. When you have decided write down the name of each resource under the correct heading.

List of resources
Wood; money; leather; nylon; eggs; records; cotton; formica; silk; cabbage; polyester; water; coal; cling wrap; paint; wheat; nail varnish; wood; sand; polythene.

Man-made resources	*Natural resources*

Many of the resources that we use the most are within ourselves. These are the *skills* and the *knowledge* we have learned throughout our lives.

Some people may be especially skilful with their hands and be helpful to others.
For example:

Think of three more examples and write them in your book. Use a sentence for each to describe how these people are helpful to others.

Some people have received training so that they can help others by giving advice and aid.
For example: doctors; solicitors.

Think of two more examples and using a sentence describe each of them in your book.

You might like to try this next part at home

Make a resource poster to display in your classroom. Collect six pictures of man-made resources and six pictures of natural resources. Divide the poster into two sections and paste the pictures of man-made resources on one section and the pictures of natural resources on the other. At the side of each picture write down a sentence explaining what it is and how it might be used.

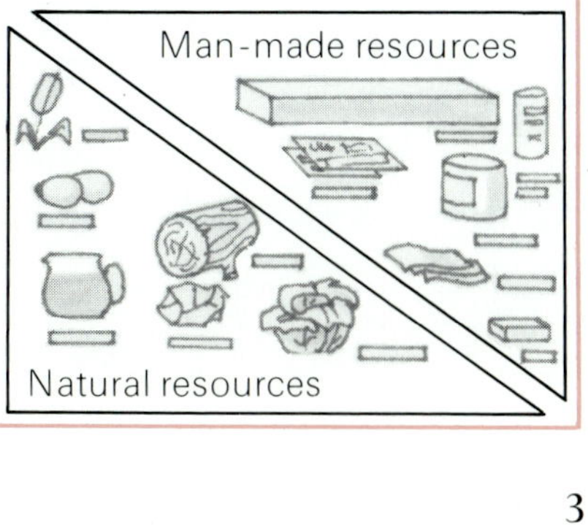

Topic 2

EXPLORING WATER

In Topic 1 you found out that water is a natural resource essential to human life. Man can survive for many weeks without food but only for a few days without water. About two-thirds of your body's weight is made up of water. Our daily intake of about one litre of water comes from solid foods as well as from drinks. You are probably used to turning on a tap for water but have you ever wondered how it gets there?

Look at the diagram below which shows how water gets from the sea to your home.

The water cycle

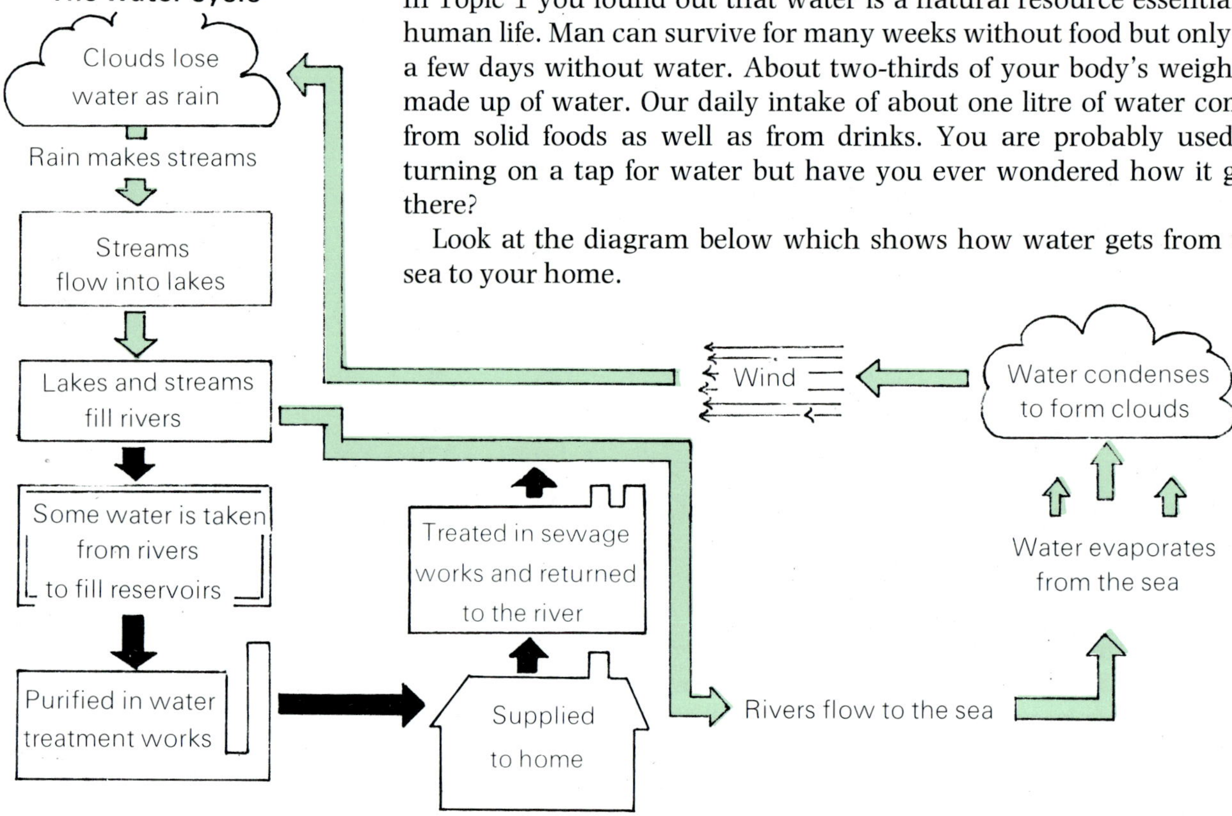

When you have studied the diagram reorganize and then write out the list below to show the correct order of stages in the water cycle.

List of stages
Waste water is treated and returned to the sea;
purified water is piped to homes;
water is collected in streams, lakes, rivers and reservoirs;
water evaporates from the sea;
water from rivers and reservoirs is purified;
clouds lose water as rain;
water condenses to form clouds.

The water authorities add a carefully measured amount of chlorine to make sure that drinking water is pure and free from any contamination. The amount of chlorine used kills any bacteria without leaving a taste.

We use water for many things besides drinks. Draw a chart like the one below and fill it in to show the many different uses of water. The pictures may give you some ideas.

Chart to show uses of water

Work in twos to complete the following experiments to find out if there is water in the foods we eat.

How much water is there in fruit and vegetables?

You will need
4 saucers
20 grams orange
20 grams apple
20 grams onion
20 grams carrot

Method
1 Draw a chart like the one below.

Food	*Weight before drying (grams)*	*Weight after drying (grams)*

2 Carefully chop the food into small pieces and place 20 grams of each food on separate saucers.
3 Complete the chart to show each food and its weight. Label each saucer with your names and the name and weight of the food.
4 Place the saucers in a drying cabinet and leave for twenty-four hours.
5 Remove the saucers from the cabinet and weigh each sample of food. Complete the chart to show the weight of each food after drying.

How much water is there in a slice of bread?

You will need
1 slice of bread (white or brown)

Method
1 Draw a chart like the one shown below.

Type of bread	*Weight before toasting (grams)*	*Weight after toasting (grams)*

2 Weigh the slice of bread and write down the weight on your chart.
3 Toast the bread on both sides to an even brown colour under a hot grill. (When you turn the bread over, you may notice steam escaping. What does this tell you?)
4 Reweigh the toasted bread on the same scales. Record this weight on your chart.

Now answer these questions using a sentence
Did the foods you used in these experiments contain water? Explain why the results of your experiments led you to this conclusion?

You might like to discuss your findings with your teacher and the rest of your class.

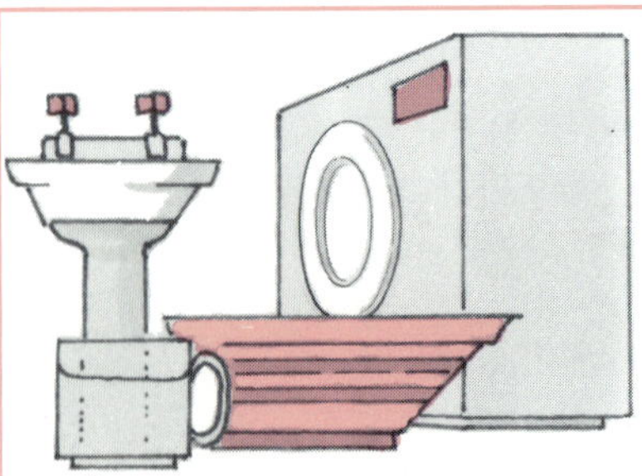

You might like to try this next part at home

Use the picture chart on page 7 to find out approximately how much water you use at home each week.

Chart to show how much water is used

Week when you collected the information:____________________

Activity	*Litres of water used*	*Number of times a week*	*Total litres of water used*
Flushing 	*40.5 litres per person per day (modern slimline cistern)*		
Cooking 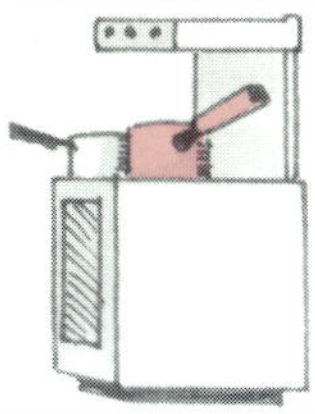	*6 litres for cooking for 4–6 people*		
Laundry 	*22.5 litres for each washing-machine load*		
Washing and bathing 	*40.5 litres per person per day*		
Drinking 	*3 litres per person per day*		
Cleaning 	*22.5 litres (or about $2\frac{1}{2}$ buckets) – enough for several cleaning tasks*		
		Total litres of water used during one week	

Topic 3 CLEANING WITH DETERGENTS

In Topic 2 you looked at some of the ways in which we use water. Now you are going to find out how water is used for cleaning. All sorts of things can be cleaned by using water.

Sometimes hot water on its own is not very good for cleaning.

In your books draw a table like the one below and list the names of some things you would add to hot water to help you to clean different things.

For cleaning	*In hot water I would add . . .*
Greasy hands	
Muddy shorts	
Dirty car	
Greasy plates	
Dirty hair	

In your table you have probably written down things like soap, shampoo and washing-up liquid. These are all examples of cleaning agents or detergents which help to remove dirt and grease from many different things. Detergents work in a special way to lift grease away from the surface of dirty materials such as metals, china, fabrics and skin.

Detergents are made up of molecules and each molecule has two parts which are quite different.

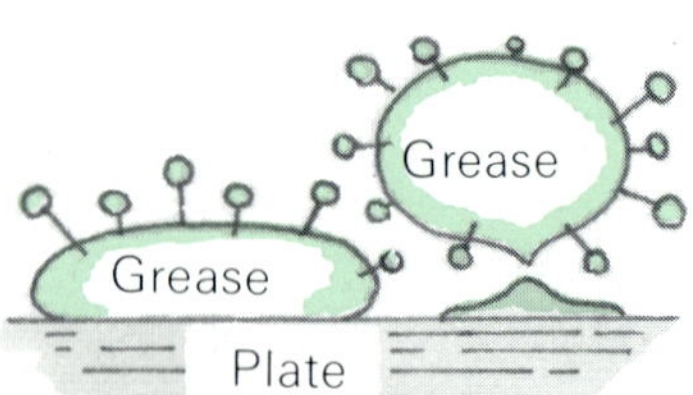

When detergent molecules are added, for example to washing-up water to clean greasy plates, the water-hating tails try to escape by pushing themselves into the grease. Gradually a droplet of grease coated with detergent molecules is formed. The grip of the grease on the plate is weakened and eventually the grease droplet is shaken free.

Work in twos to complete the experiment.

Experiment to find out how cold and hot water with detergent added can help to clean greasy plates

You will need
4 small china plates
1 palette knife
2 teaspoons margarine
2 washing-up bowls
liquid washing-up detergent
4 circles of filter paper
1 draining rack
1 tea towel

Method
1 Use the palette knife to smear the centre of each plate with some of the margarine.
2 In your books, draw a table like the one started here to record your results.

Plates smeared with margarine	*What I did*	*What happened*	*Mark out of 5 for cleanliness (5 = highest)*
1			
2			

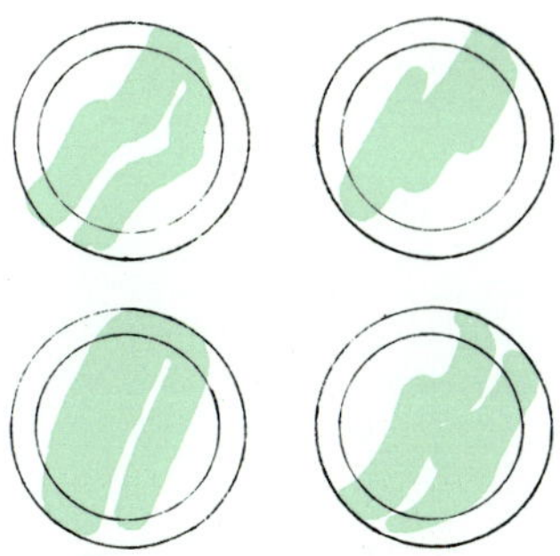

3 Half fill one of the washing-up bowls with hand-hot water and the other with cold water.
4 Take one of the plates and swish it from side to side in the bowl of cold water. Look carefully at what happens then lift out the plate and leave it to drain in the rack.

Swish plates from side to side – don't rub the surface

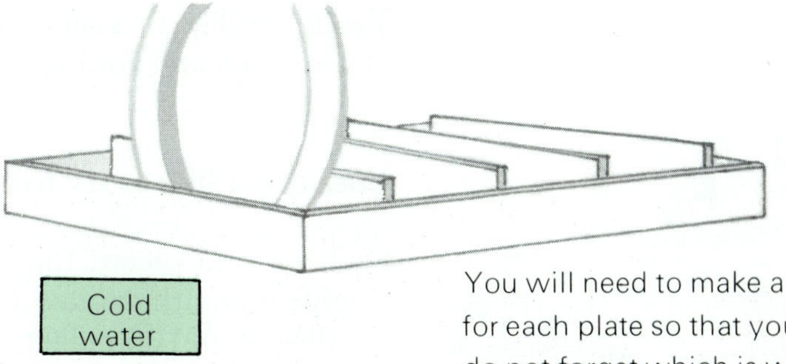

You will need to make a label for each plate so that you do not forget which is which!

5 Take another plate and swish it from side to side in the hand-hot water. Look carefully at what happens then lift this plate out and leave it to drain.
6 To each washing-up bowl of water add one short squeeze of liquid washing-up detergent. Swish around the water in each bowl to mix in the liquid and notice what happens.
7 Take the third plate and swish it from side to side in the bowl of cold water with detergent added. Look carefully at what happens then lift out the plate and leave it to drain.
8 Take the last plate and swish it from side to side in the hand-hot water with detergent added. Look carefully at what happens and then lift out this plate and leave it to drain.
9

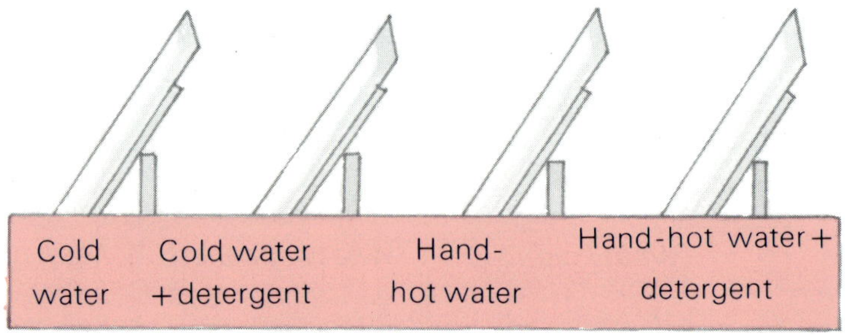

Carefully examine and make a label for each plate. Write down on your results chart what has happened to each of the plates.
10 Take one circle of filter paper and rub it over the centre of one of the plates. Do this three more times using a new filter paper for each plate.

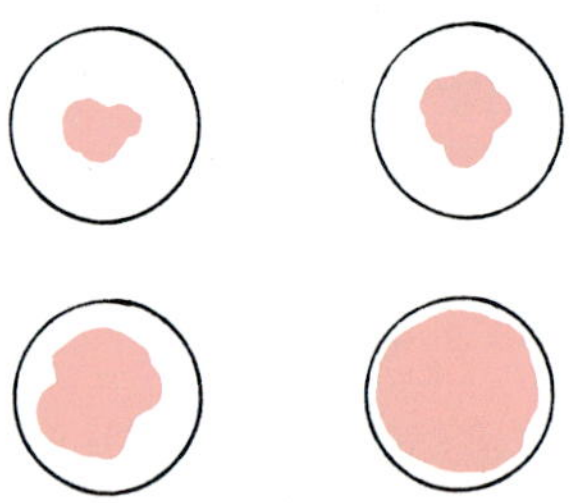

Then carefully examine and compare the four circles of paper to see how much grease has been absorbed (soaked up).
11 Using the results of the filter paper test complete the results chart by giving a mark out of 5 for each method of cleaning.
12 Finally clear up, using the method which you thought worked best to wash up all the equipment you have used.

You might like to discuss the results of your experiment with the rest of your class and your teacher.

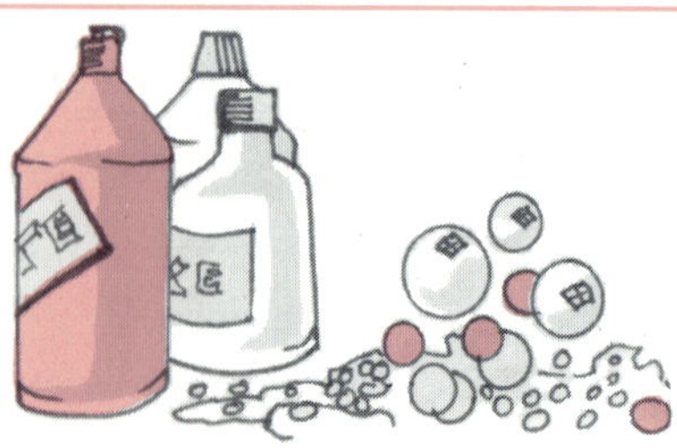

You might like to try this next part at home

Find out and record the cost of six brands of liquid washing-up detergent and the amount of liquid that each contains. Then work out the cost of 100 millilitres of each liquid. Present your findings in the form of a chart.

Topic 4

CLEANING CLOTHES

In Topic 3 you found out how detergents help to clean dishes. In this topic you will investigate how detergents work to clean clothes.

If you examine closely a woven fabric you will see that it is made up of two yarns. The yarns have been interlaced or woven so that they hold together to make the fabric. Clothes get dirty or soiled even during storage but especially when they are worn.

If you looked closely at the fabric under a microscope you would see:

that grease and dirt particles are trapped in between the yarns;

that stains have soaked into or penetrated the yarns.

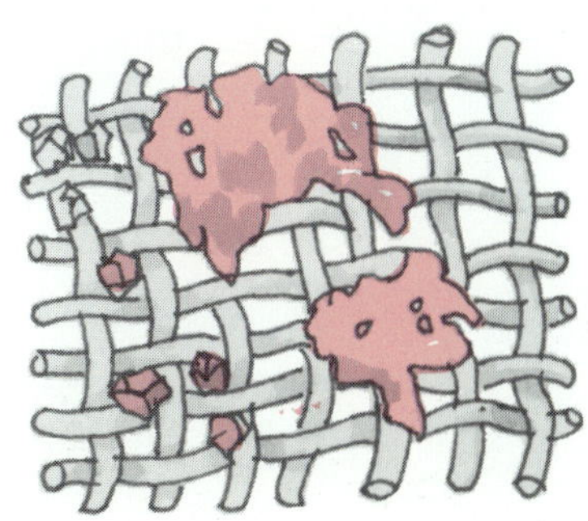

When clothes are washed the water has to wet the fabric by penetrating into and between the yarns to lift out the dirt and stains.

Work in twos to complete this experiment.

Experiment to find out if water alone will wet fabrics

You will need
1 glass rod
1 piece of felt, 15 cms × 15 cms
liquid detergent
powder detergent
1 small basin, half-full of cold water

Method
1 Draw a chart like the one shown here to record your results.

Subject	What I did to them	What happened to the water drops	What happened to the cloth underneath
6 drops of water			
2 drops of water			
2 drops of water			
2 drops of water			

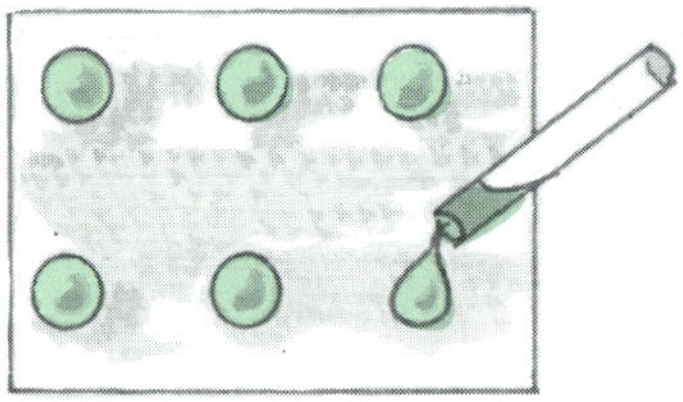

2 Lay the fabric flat on a table (if it is creased, press with a warm iron ⏚).
3 Using the glass rod allow six single drops of water to fall onto the fabric. Make sure the drops are evenly spaced as shown in the picture.
4 Look carefully at the drops of water. Now pick up one corner of the fabric and watch what happens to the drops of water. Record on your chart what happens.
5 Shake the fabric vigorously to remove the droplets of water.
6 Lay the fabric flat on the table again and use the glass rod to place six more drops of water on the fabric.
7 Leave two of the drops of water untouched.
Use the glass rod to add one single drop of liquid detergent to two of the drops of water. Look carefully to see what happens. To the last two drops add a sprinkle of detergent powder. Look carefully to see what happens. Record all your results on your chart.

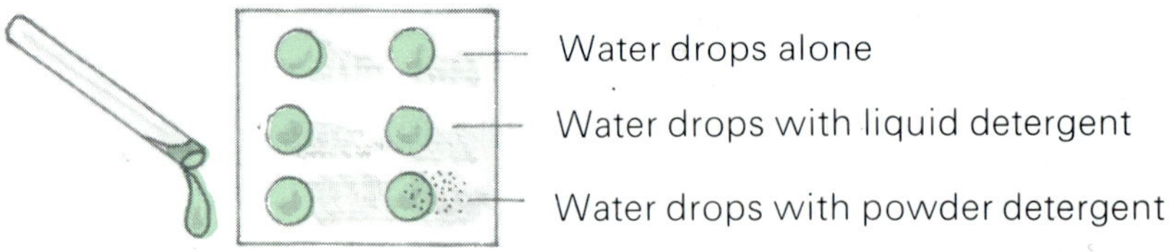

8 Look at the fabric beneath each drop to see which part of the fabric is wettest. Record this on your chart.

You probably noticed that water on its own formed a well-rounded drop on the fabric – almost as if each drop had an invisible skin around it. Water molecules have a strong attraction for each other and when they stick together in this way a *surface tension* or skin is formed. However, if detergent molecules are added to the water the surface tension is broken and the drop of water collapses, spreads out and soaks into the fabric. The surface tension is broken because the detergent molecules have pushed in between the water molecules and weakened the attraction between them.

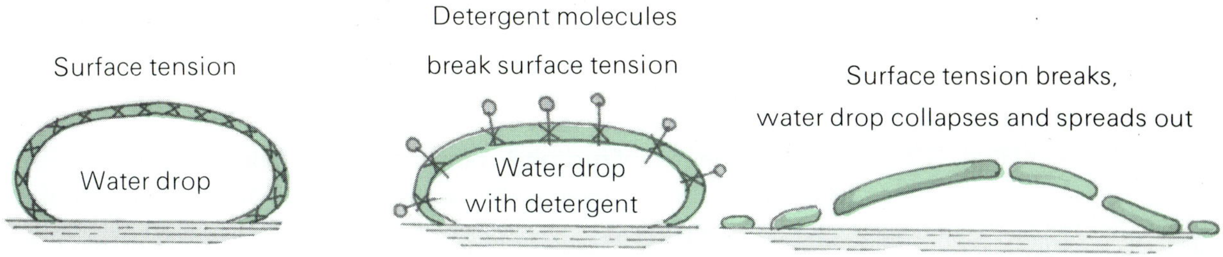

Therefore one reason for using detergents is to help water to wet clothes.

Work in twos to complete this next experiment.

Experiment to find out the best way of removing grease stains from cotton calico

You will need

5 pieces of cotton calico, 8 cms × 8 cms
4 straight pins
2 absorbent paper kitchen towels
200 mls of cold water
200 mls of hot (not boiling) water
2 teaspoons of powder detergent
1 glass rod
4 basins
4 teaspoons
a little cooking oil

Method

1 Draw a chart like the one shown overleaf to record your results.

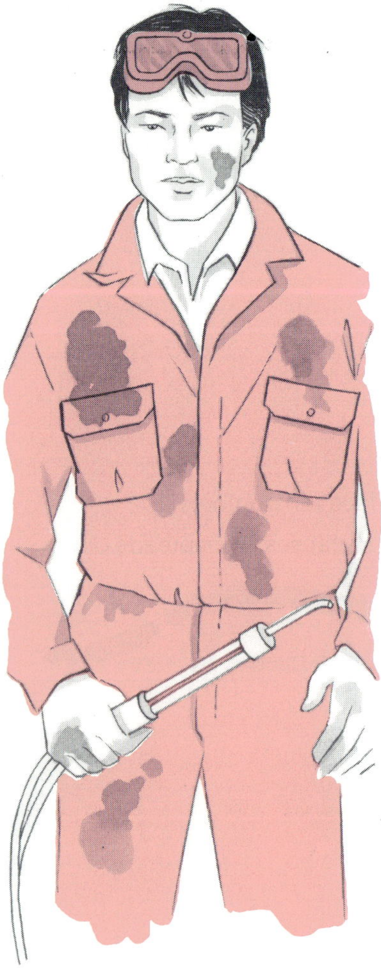

Samples of fabric	What I did	What happened to the oil stain	Mark out of 5 (5 = highest, 1 = lowest)
Control			
Cold water			
Hot water			
Cold water + detergent			
Hot water + detergent			

2 Lay the five fabric pieces on the table and in the centre of each put two drops of cooking oil.
3 Put aside one of the fabric pieces as this will be a control.
4 Prepare the basins of water as shown in the picture below and label each one clearly.

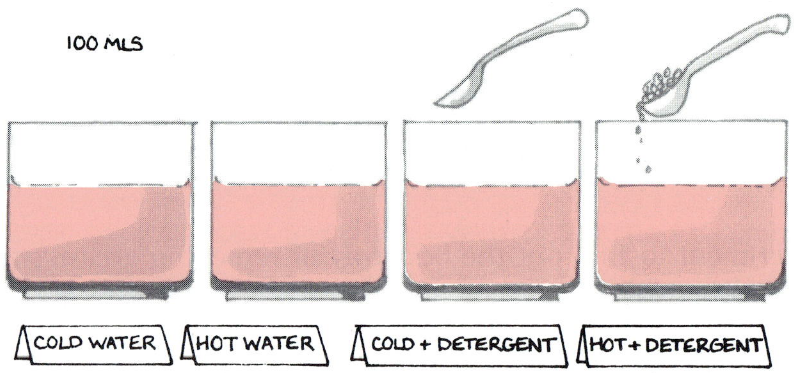

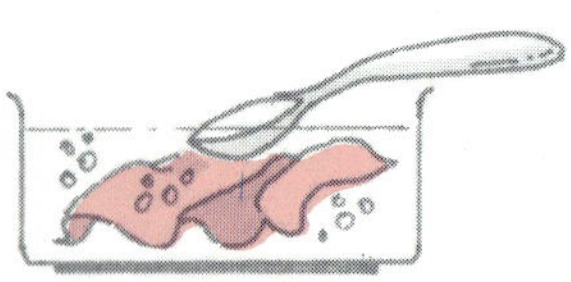

COLD	HOT
COLD + DETERGENT	HOT + DETERGENT

5 Put one piece of fabric in each basin and using a teaspoon, move the fabric around for about 5 to 10 seconds. Leave the fabric pieces to soak while you prepare the paper towel and fill in the first column of your chart.
6 Draw lines on the towel to make 4 boxes as shown. Use a ball point pen to label each box.
7 Lift the fabric out of the water by one of the corners and shake well. Pin each fabric piece to the correct box on the paper towel and leave to dry in a warm place. Press with a warm iron.

8 Compare the four washed pieces with the control. Describe what you see on your chart.
9 Complete your results chart by giving a mark out of 5 for cleanness.

You might like to discuss your results with your class and with your teacher.

In this experiment the detergent molecule has worked in the same way as it did in Topic 3.

Grease stain on fabric

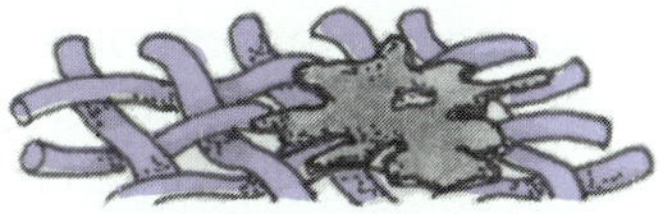

Water-hating tails of detergent molecule push into grease

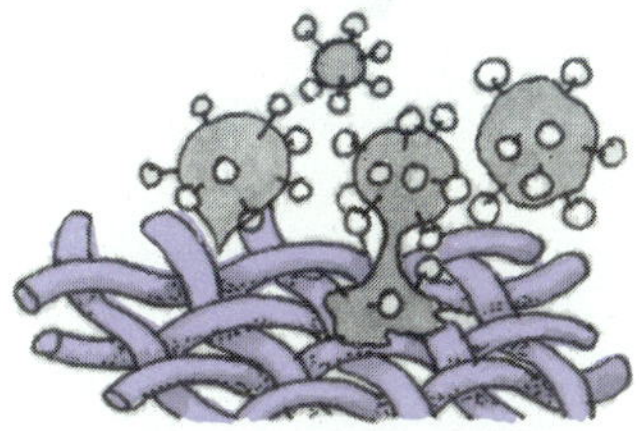

Grease is lifted out of the fabric

Some detergents are made especially to work in cold water whilst others work best in hot water. However some fabrics cannot be washed in hot water – so it is important to choose the right washing temperature for each type of fabric. One way of doing this is to look at the wash-care label inside clothes as this will tell you how they should be washed.
For example:

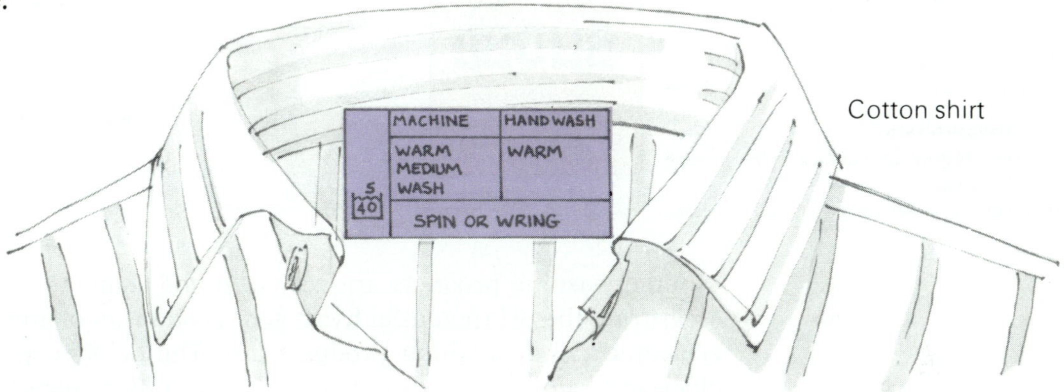

Cotton shirt

Look back at Topic 14 in Book 1 to remind you of these wash-care codes.

You might like to try this next part at home

Choose two outer garments which you wear regularly and look for the wash-care code on each one. In a paragraph write down how you would follow the code instructions to clean each of these garments. There is usually a guide to all of the wash-care codes on the side of commercial powder detergent packets which will help you. If you like you could cut out the fabric-care guide from an empty detergent packet and stick it in your book.

Topic 5

CHOOSING A WASHING PRODUCT

There are many different types of washing products to choose from. Often they are in the form of a powder though they can be concentrated liquids or flakes. They all contain either soap or detergent or a mixture of both along with many other chemicals especially designed to deal with different washing problems. With so much choice it is easy to choose a powder which is not suitable for either a particular fabric or for the particular dirt and stains.

Here is a picture of a packet of washing powder and a list of what it is likely to contain.

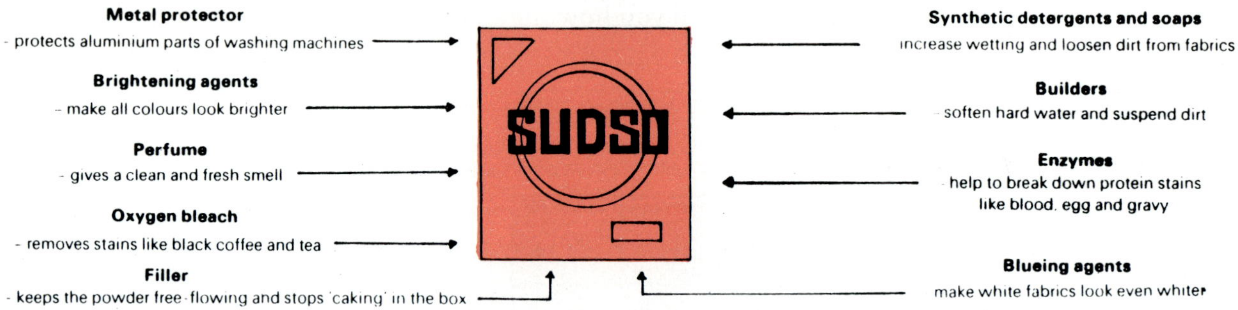

Some washing products are very acid and some are very alkaline. Measuring the pH (potential hydrogen) is one way of finding out how acid or alkaline washing products are. The acidity or alkalinity of different products is measured on a pH scale which starts at 0 and goes up to 14.

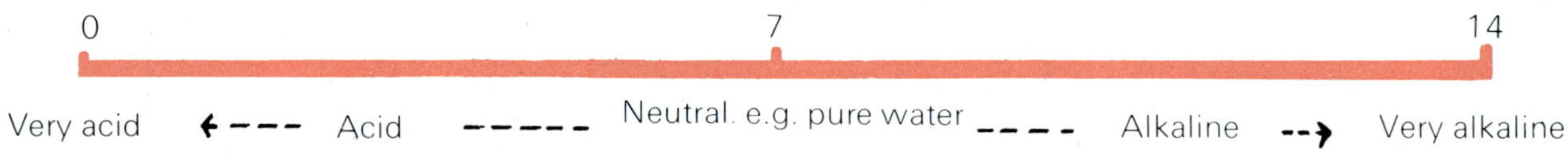

A pH scale

To measure pH a special indicator paper is used. The paper changes colour; the extent to which this happens depends on the amount of acid or alkali that the substance being tested contains. The colour change is then compared against a colour chart. Most science departments have indicator paper for pH testing.

Washing products which are alkaline (pH above 7) are good for removing grease stains. However alkaline products can damage delicate fabrics such as wool.

Some washing products have a neutral pH and can be used for delicate fabrics and for fabrics with special finishes.

Knowing the pH of different washing products can help you to choose the right product for the right fabric.

Work in twos to complete this experiment.

Experiment to find out the pH of different washing products

You will need

1 teaspoon of each of the following washing products:
- mild liquid washing product
- enzyme or biological powder
- whiter than white, stain removal product
- mild soap flake product

5 small basins
cold water
a tablespoon
pH indicator paper with colour chart
sellotape

Method

1 Draw a chart like the one shown here to record your results.

Washing product tested	*Indicator paper used (tape on to chart)*	*pH of product*

2 Next make five labels as shown here:
- i cold water;
- ii cold water and liquid washing product;
- iii cold water and biological product;
- iv cold water and whiter than white, synthetic detergent powder;
- v cold water and soap flakes.

3 Place the five basins on a table and follow the pictures below to prepare each product for testing. To each of these basins add 4 tablespoons of cold water and 1 tablespoon of each product according to the label.

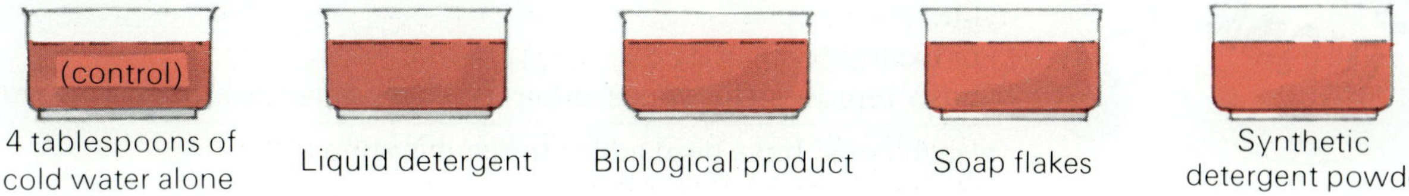

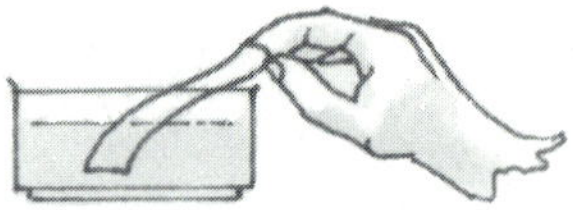

4 Make sure your hands are absolutely dry then take a piece of indicator paper and dip one end in the basin of cold water.
5 Compare the colour of the wet end of the paper with the colour chart and decide on the pH.
6 Use the tape to secure the dry end of the paper to your results chart.
7 Repeat the indicator test for each of the remaining four basins. Each time carefully compare the wet end of the indicator paper to the colour chart and decide on the pH. Tape each of the indicator papers to your results chart and complete the rest of the chart.
8 Draw a scale like the one shown here and write down the name of each product tested against the pH you decided on.
9 Finally answer these questions in your book using a sentence.

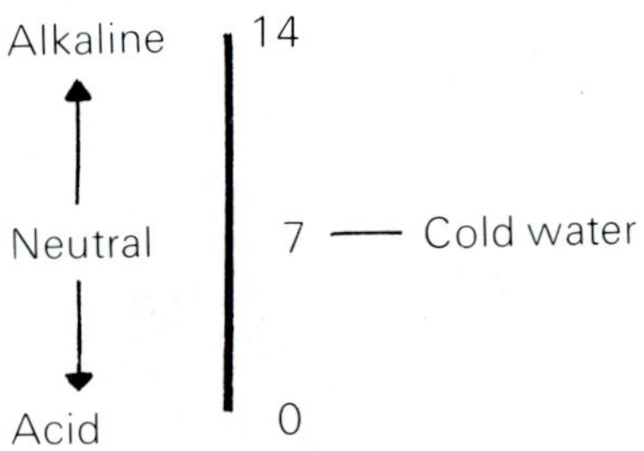

pH scale of washing products that were tested

- Explain which of the washing products you tested would be suitable for:

removing grease from a tea towel;
removing gravy stains from a tablecloth;
washing a delicate wool sweater.

You might like to discuss your results with the rest of your class and your teacher.

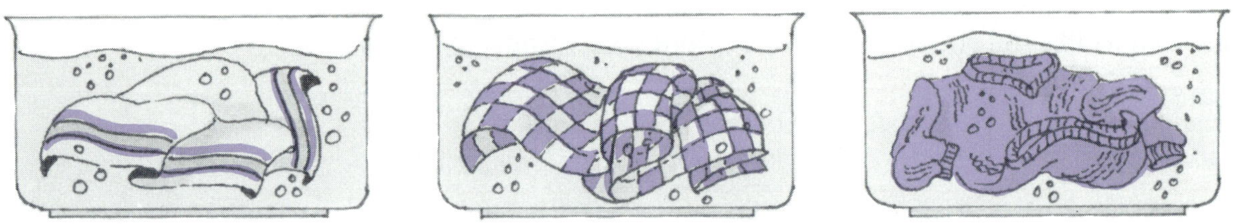

You might like to try this next part at home

Read the information on the packets of the washing products usually used in your home, to find out what they are especially designed to do.

Then write out a list of the selling slogans which the manufacturers use to sell their particular product. At the side of each slogan write down the name of a substance which the manufacturer might have added to make the product special in this way. Use the picture of a packet of washing powder at the beginning of this topic to help you.

For example:
Sudso removes the stains other powders leave behind – Oxygen bleach could have been added to remove stains.

FINDING OUT HOW HEAT TRAVELS

Topic 6

Heat is a resource we use to: cook food;
heat water;
heat rooms.

Heat is a form of energy which can travel from one point to another. In this topic you are going to investigate the three different ways in which heat can travel.

Conduction

Conduction is one of the ways that heat can travel.

All solid materials are made up of tiny molecules. When the molecules are heated they vibrate or rub together so that heat is conducted or passed on from one molecule to the next.

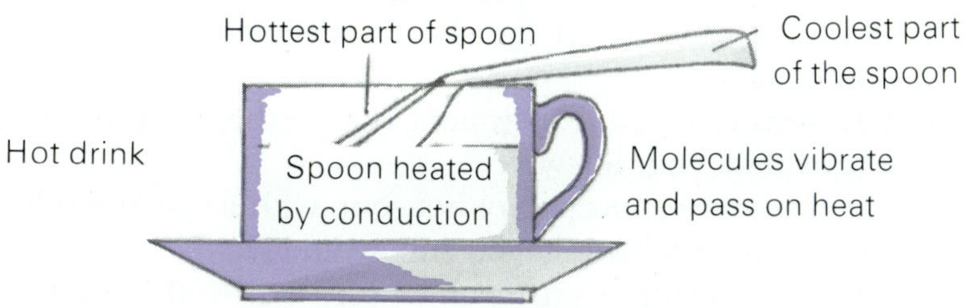

Some solid materials conduct heat from one molecule to the next very quickly – these materials are called good conductors.

Other materials are called poor conductors because they conduct heat very slowly.

Work in twos to complete this experiment.

Experiment to find out which material is the best conductor of heat

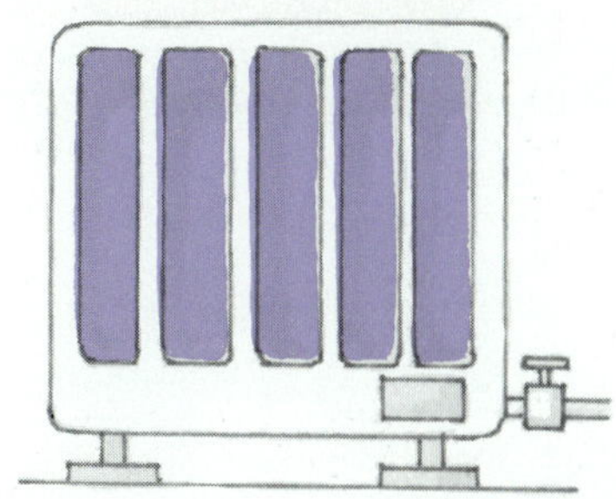

You will need

1 500 ml plastic measuring jug
300 ml of boiling water
1 metal dessert spoon
1 plastic dessert spoon
1 plastic spatula
1 wooden spoon
(spoons made from different materials)

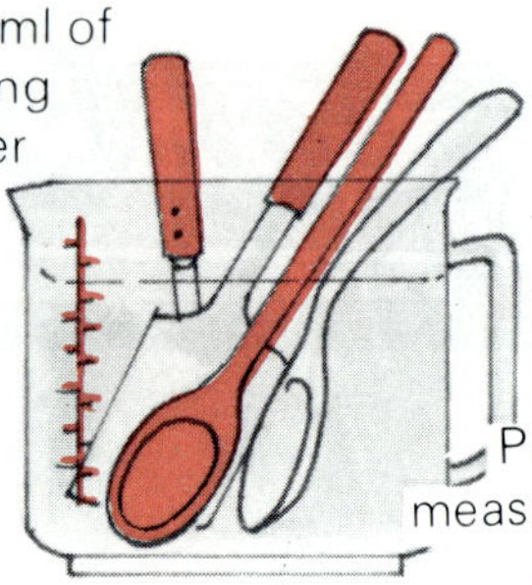

Method

1 Place the jug on a tray in case of spillage. You will be using boiling water so – *take care*.

2 Put all the spoons and the spatula into the jug with their handles sticking out.

3 Fill the measuring jug up to the 300 ml mark with boiling water. Leave for 10 minutes.

4 In your book draw a chart like the one started here to record your results.

Types of material	*Cool* ✓	*Warm* ✓	*Hot* ✓	*Very hot* ✓
Wooden spoon				
Plastic spoon				

5 Now, carefully feel each handle to find out if it is cool, warm, hot or very hot. Then put a tick on the chart under one of the headings to record your results.

6 Using the results of your experiment answer these questions using a sentence to explain your answer.

- If you had to stir a saucepan of hot soup with a spoon while it was cooking which material would you choose and why?
- If you were choosing a saucepan to use, which of these would be best and why?

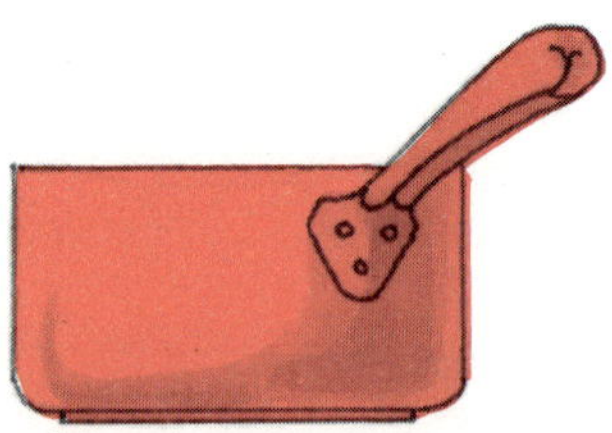
Metal saucepan with metal handle

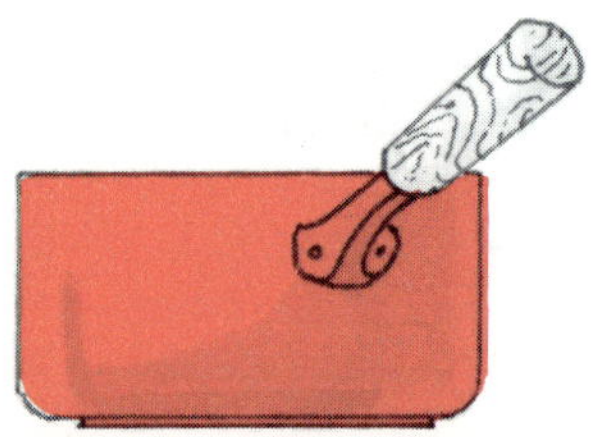
Metal saucepan with wooden handle

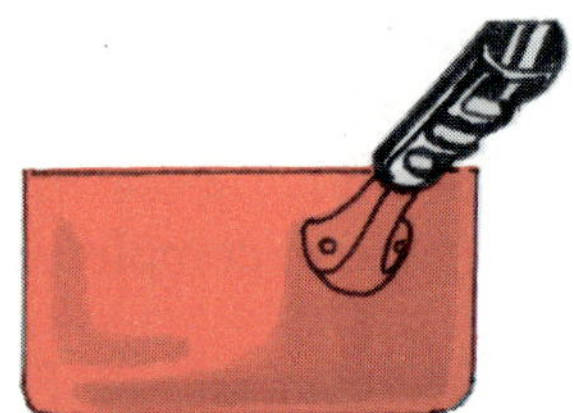
Metal saucepan with plastic handle

Convection

Convection is another way that heat can travel.

In liquids such as water, or gases such as air, heat travels by convection. As the molecules in the gas or liquid are heated they expand and rise and cooler molecules sink down to take their place.

The falling and rising of the molecules cause *convection currents*.

An oven is heated by *convection currents*.

A room is heated by *convection currents*.

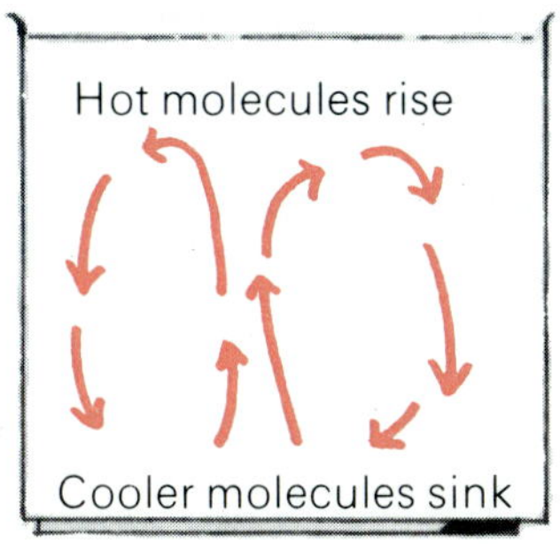

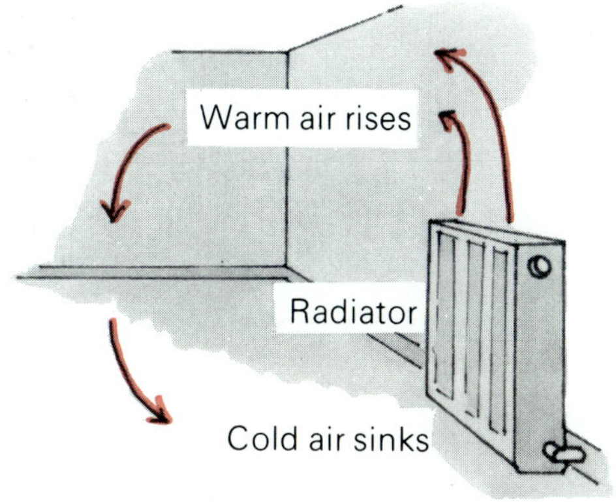

Radiation

Another way that heat travels is by *radiation.*

The sun heats the earth by radiation. An electric fire heats your body by radiation.

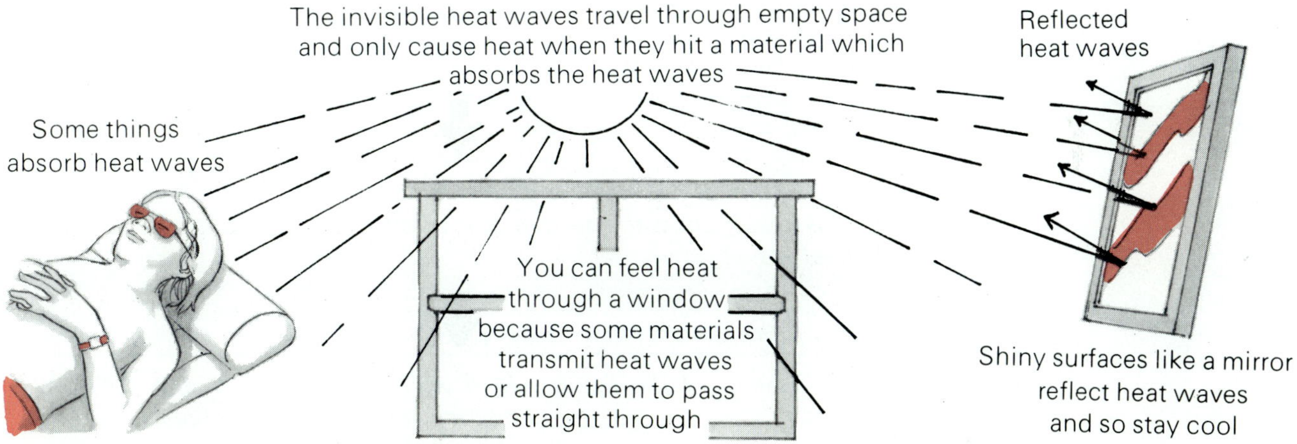

Radiation is used in grilling to heat food.
Work in twos to complete this experiment.

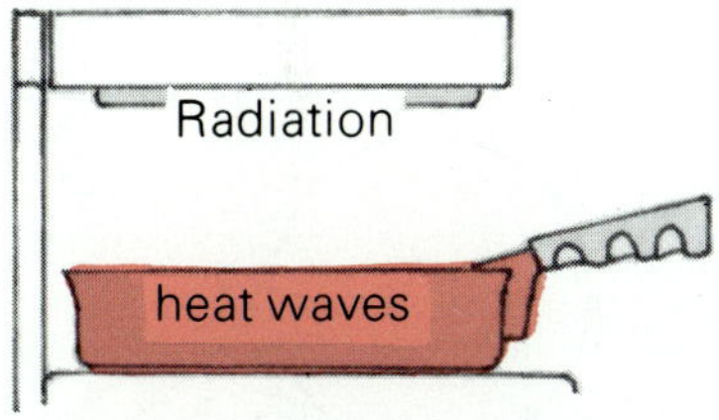

Experiment to find out if shiny surfaces reflect radiant heat waves

You will need

1 slice of white bread
1 strip of foil, 4 cms × 16 cms

Method

1 Lay the foil strip, with the shiny side uppermost, over the slice of bread.

2 Place the bread on a grill rack under a hot grill. Leave until the uncovered parts of the bread are quite brown.

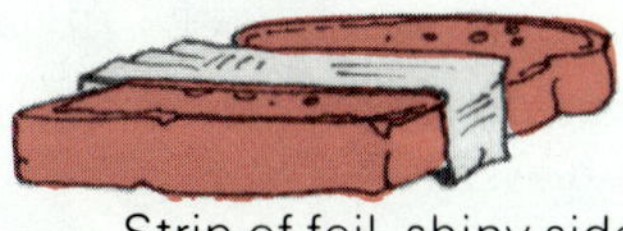

Tuck the ends of the foil under the slice of bread

3 Remove the bread from under the grill. Remove the foil strip and look carefully to see what has happened.
4 In your book draw a flow chart like the one shown below. Fill in the chart to explain the results of your experiment as it progresses.

Flow chart showing the results of the experiment to find out if shiny surfaces reflect radiant heat waves

A slice of bread was covered in part by a foil strip, and placed under a hot grill for several minutes.
Draw a picture of what the bread looked like.

↓

After several minutes the bread was taken out from under the grill and the foil strip removed.
Draw a picture of what the bread looked like.

↓

The colour of the bread under the foil strip was________________. This result showed me that shiny foil________________ radiant heat waves.

↓

The colour of the bread which was not covered by the foil strip was________________. This result showed me that bread ________________radiant heat waves.

You might like to try this next part at home

Look at each of the pictures below and describe what would happen on a hot sunny day to the following.

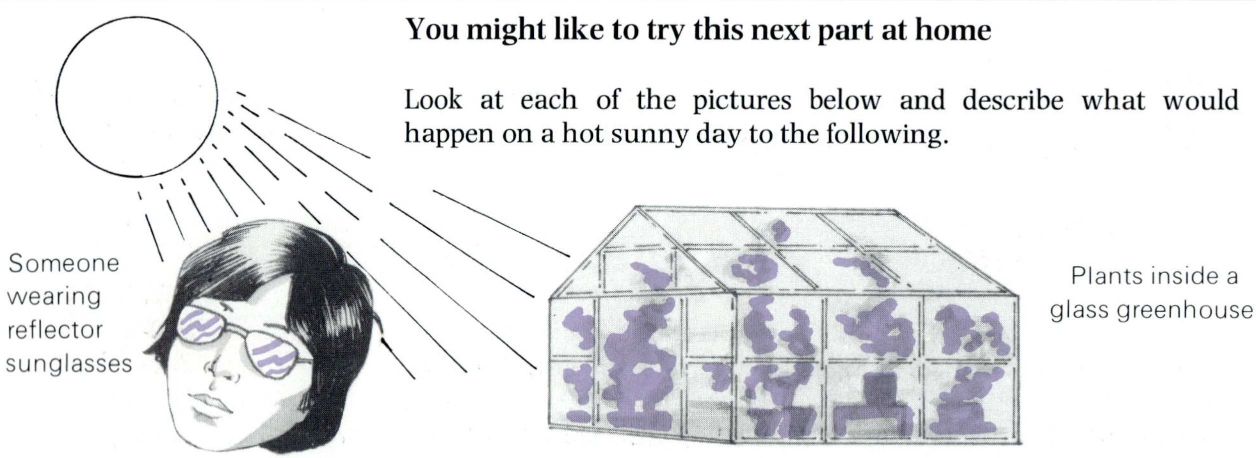

CONSERVING HEAT

Topic 7

In Topic 6 you discovered that heat can travel from one point to another by conduction, convection and radiation.

In this topic you are going to find out how the movement of heat from one point to another can be slowed down so that: homes stay warmer; drinks stay hotter for longer.

Keeping a home warm

In a cold climate a lot of money is spent on heating buildings. Buildings can be heated by: oil heaters; electricity; coal; gas; central heating.

Look at picture A which shows how heat is lost, or travels away from a house by: *conduction* – through walls and windows; *convection* – up chimneys and above the roof; *radiation* – in all directions.

Heat loss from buildings can be prevented by using insulating materials which stop or certainly slow down heat travel.

Look at picture B to see how insulation materials can help to prevent heat loss from a house.

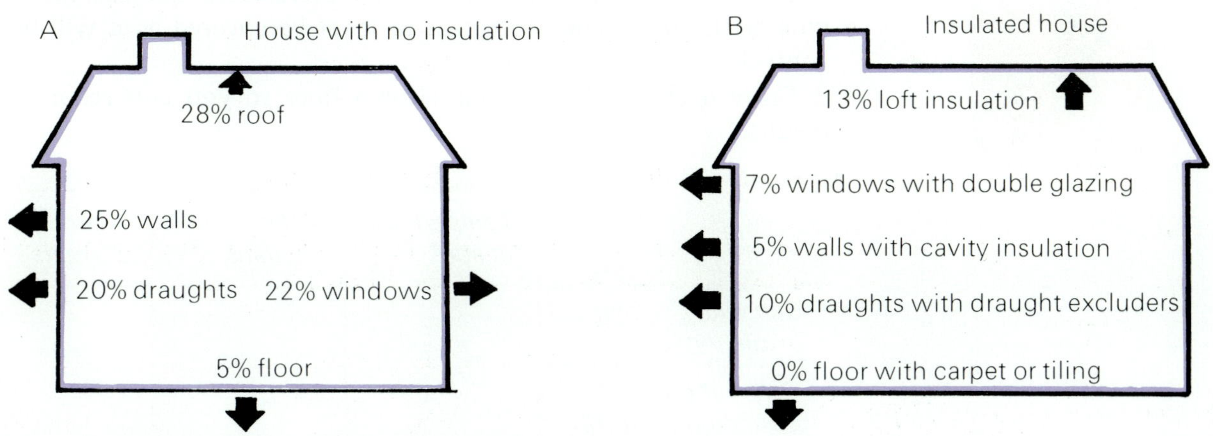

Look very carefully at the figures for the uninsulated house.

Draw a chart like the one shown overleaf then write a list of the ways in which heat can be lost from a building. Start your list with the way that loses the most heat and so on. In the last column of the chart write down the % of heat that can be saved if the house is insulated.

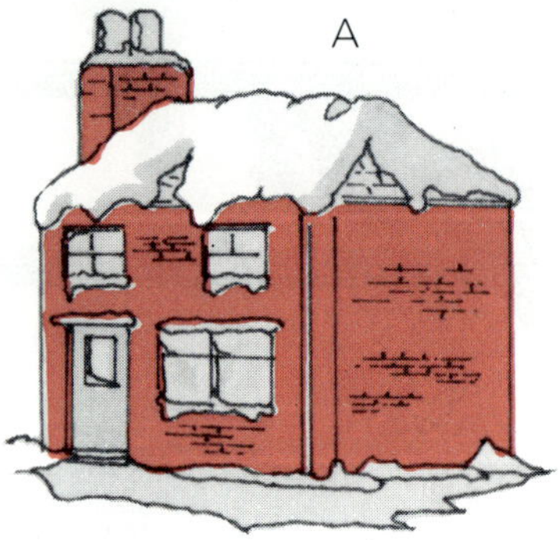

How heat is lost from a house	Uninsulated – % of heat lost	Insulated – % of heat saved

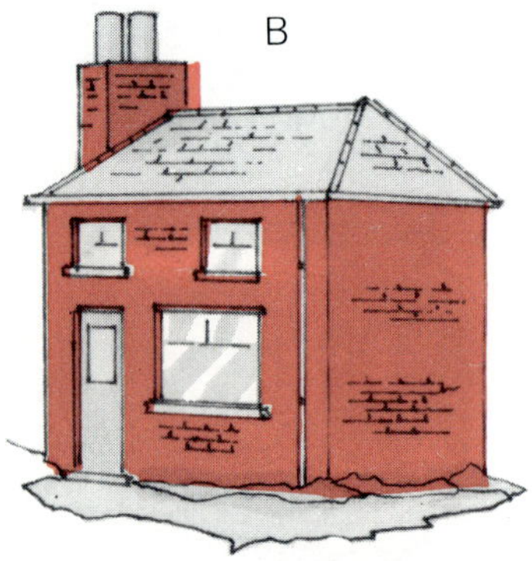

Because hot air rises a lot of heat can be lost from the roof of a house, especially if it is not insulated.

Here is a picture of the roofs of two houses after snowy weather.

● Which of the two houses pictured in the margin has loft insulation? In your book write a sentence to explain your answer.

Work in twos to complete this experiment.

Experiment to find out if loft insulation material prevents heat loss

You will need

2 empty soft drinks cans (make sure they are both the same)
2 centigrade thermometers (longer than the height of the can – about 26 cm)
Hot, but *not* boiling, water
1 piece of loft insulating material cut to 12 cms × 26 cms
straight pins or sellotape.

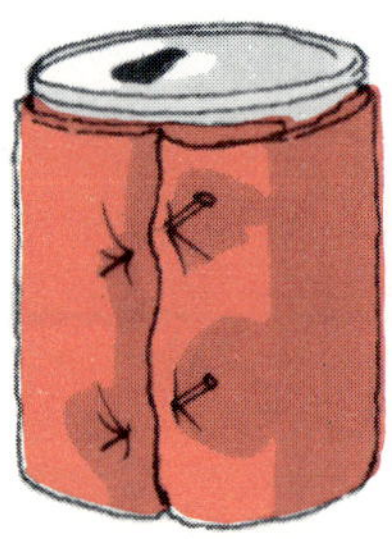

Method

1 Cover one can with the insulating material and hold this firm with pins or the tape. The other can will not be covered as it will be the control.
2 Draw a chart like the one shown here so you can record your results.

	Temperature at start	After 15 mins	After 30 mins
Can with insulation			
Can without insulation (control)			

3 Very carefully fill both cans with the hot water, using a measuring jug. Place both cans in a cold place, such as on a window ledge.
4 Using the hole left by the ring-pull insert a thermometer into each can. Record these temperatures on the chart.

5 Take the temperature of each can again after 15 minutes and then after 30 minutes and record these on the chart.

Which can stayed hottest for the longest time?

At the end of the experiment write a paragraph to describe what you noticed about the temperature of each can once it had been left in a cool place.

Keeping drinks hot for a longer time

One way of keeping drinks hot is to use a vacuum flask. Look at the picture below to find out how a vacuum flask prevents heat loss.

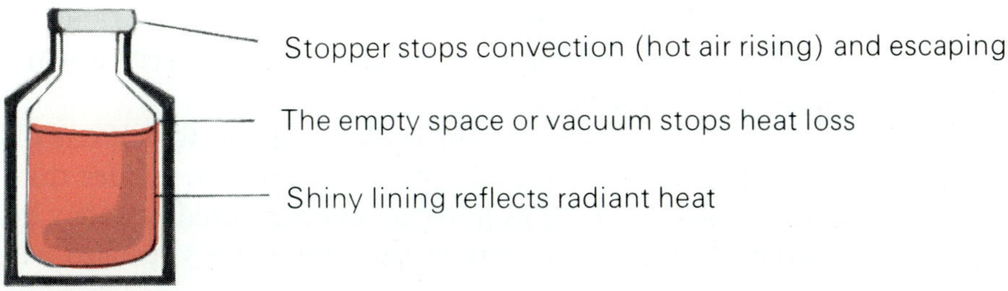

Trapped air between layers of paper is also used to keep foods hot or cold as air is a poor conductor.

Fish and chips
Trapped air stops heat escaping

Ice cream

Trapped air stops cold escaping and heat getting to the inside

Polystyrene is a plastic foam. Air is trapped in between the plastic molecules and this makes polystyrene a poor conductor of heat.

Polystyrene is used to keep things hot and cold.

Work in twos to complete this experiment.

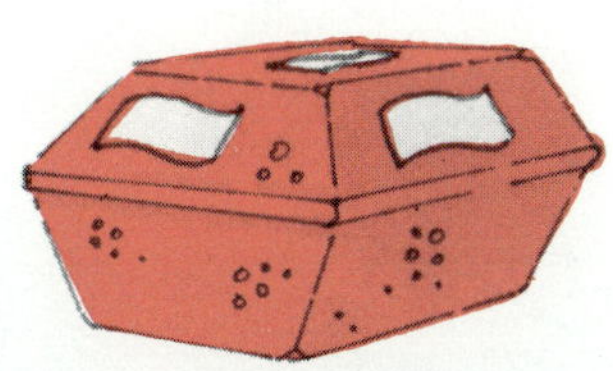

Hamburgers kept hot in polystyrene box

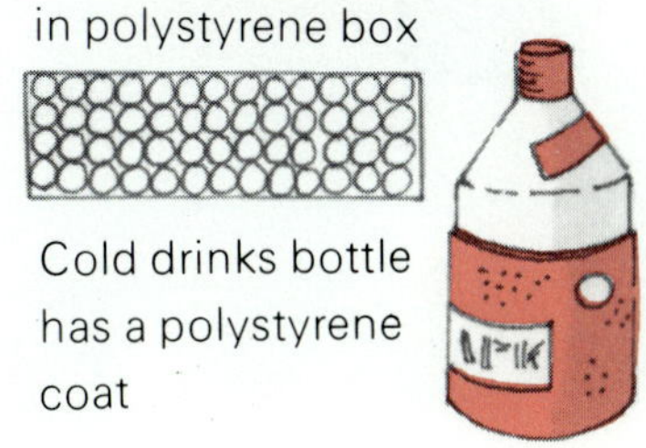

Cold drinks bottle has a polystyrene coat

Experiment to find the best material for cups in a hot drink vending machine

You will need
1 thin plastic cup
1 polystyrene cup
1 centigrade thermometer
hot, but *not* boiling, water

Method

1 Draw a chart like the one shown here.

Type of cup	*Temperature at start*	*After 5 mins*	*After 10 mins*

2 Half fill each cup with the hot water. Lift up each cup with your hand and then write down which feels the hottest to the touch.

3 Use the thermometer to take the temperature of the water in each cup: at the start; after 5 minutes; after 10 minutes.

Record these results on your chart.

4 After 10 minutes lift up the cups again and write down which feels the hottest to the touch.

Write a paragraph in your book to explain which one of these cups you would choose and why, if you wanted to ensure that: the drink stayed hot for as long as possible; the cup could be safely held without burning the hand (remember that the water you used was not quite boiling).

INVESTIGATING ELECTRICITY Topic 8

Electricity is energy which can be used to:

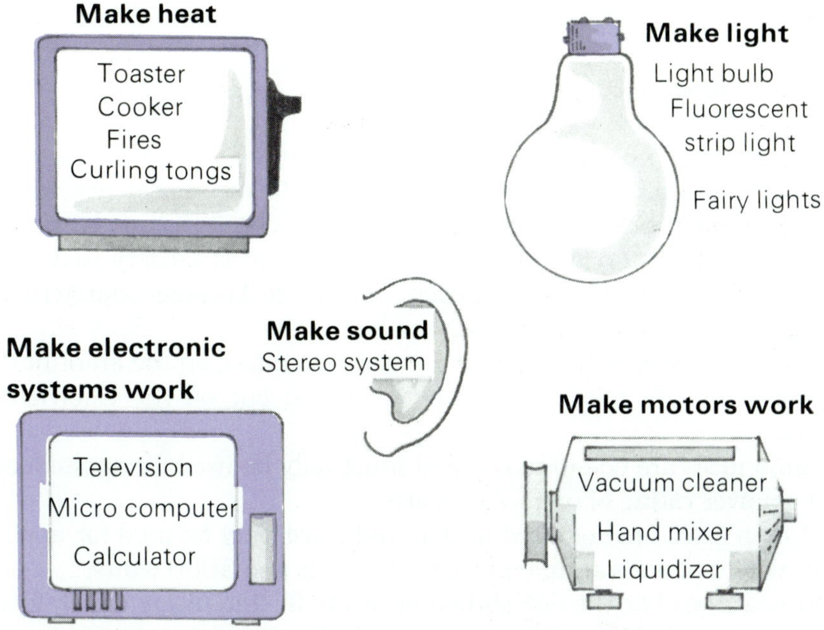

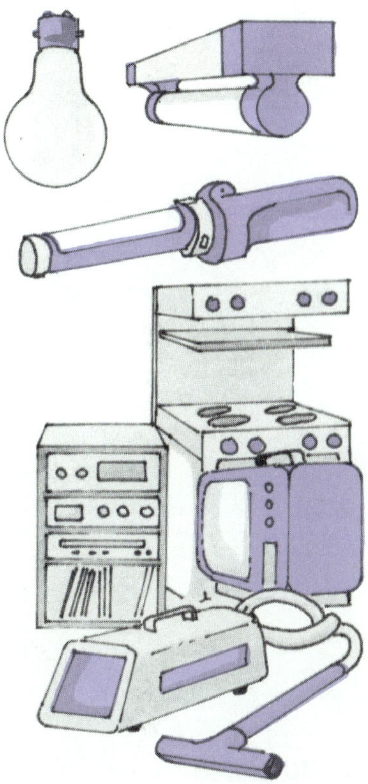

Make a list in your books of the ways in which you use electricity. For example: I use electricity when . . . I make toast/I play a record.

The power of electricity is measured in *watts* (W). One thousand watts (1000) are called a kilowatt (kW). Electrical equipment needs a certain number of watts to work.

For example: hair curling tongs – 20 watts; light bulb – 100 watts; vacuum cleaner – 900 watts; portable black and white TV – 12 watts; fluorescent strip light – 40 watts; cooker – 12 000 watts; stereo cassette – 30 watts.

Each piece of electrical equipment has a metal information plate attached to it. If you look carefully at this special *rating plate* attached to appliances you will see the *power rating* or number of watts that the equipment needs to work.

Electricity helps us in our lives, however if it is used incorrectly it can be very dangerous.

Electricity can cause: fires; electric shocks.

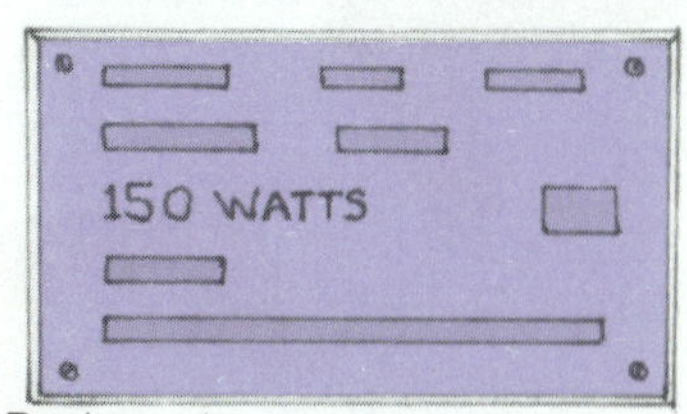

Rating plate on a mixer shows that this appliance needs 150 watts to work. So the power rating of this mixer is 150 watts.

The safety rules which should always be followed

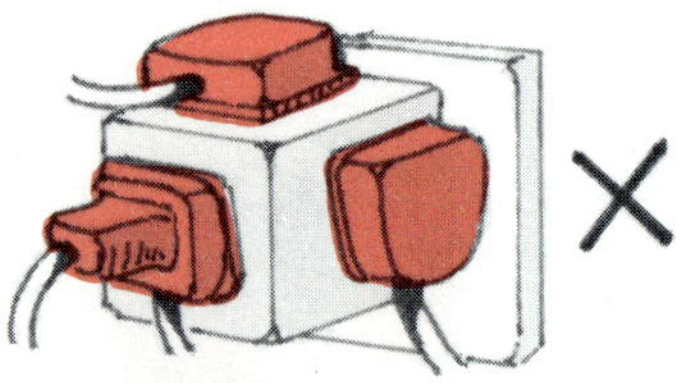

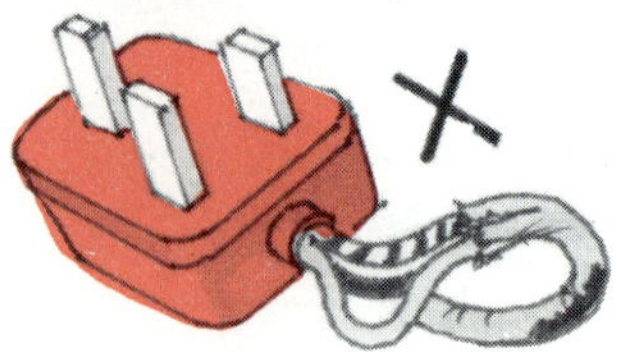

1 Electricity and water are a fatal combination.
Do not handle plugs with wet hands and never take any portable electric appliances into the bathroom.
2 Do not overload adaptors.
3 Do not use equipment if the wire or cord is frayed.
4 All plugs must be correctly wired and fitted with the right size of fuse – never wire plugs unless you know exactly what you are doing and are supervised by a trained person.

What is a fuse?

A fuse is a very important safety device. Fuses are found inside electric plugs and inside consumer units (main fuse boxes). Fuses are wires which will melt or fuse so that the flow of electricity is cut off if the electric current is too great. So in a way fuses act as a safety switch – cutting off the supply of electricity before it becomes dangerous enough to damage the appliance.

Plug fuses are mostly 3 amp or 13 amp depending on the amount of current they will take before they melt and cut off the electricity supply.

3 amp fuses are coloured red and must only be used for appliances with a power rating of up to 720 watts.

13 amp fuses are coloured brown and must only be used for appliances with a power rating between 720 watts and 3000 watts.

Draw a chart like the one shown here and fill it in to say which fuse you would need to use with each of the appliances pictured below.

List of equipment and power rating	*Type of fuse needed*

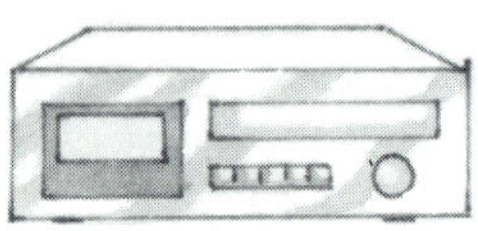

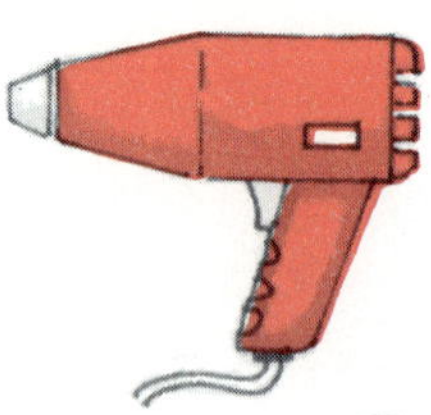

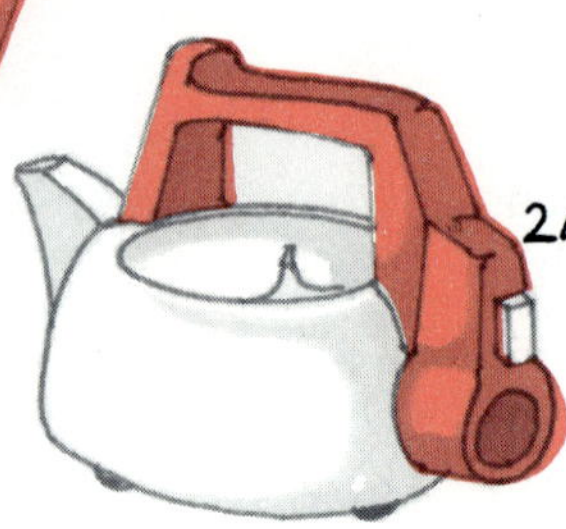

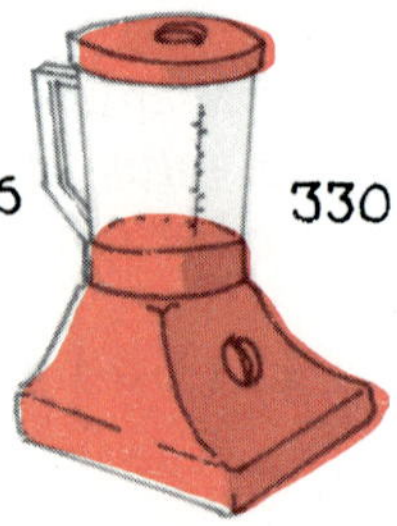

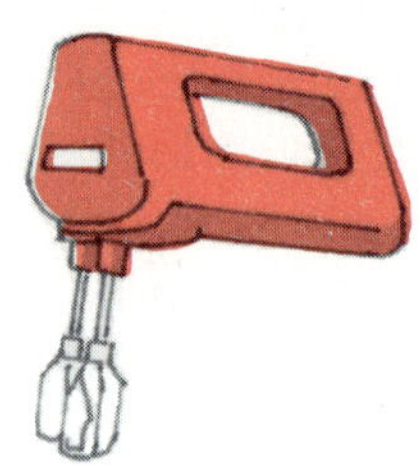

A three-pin plug

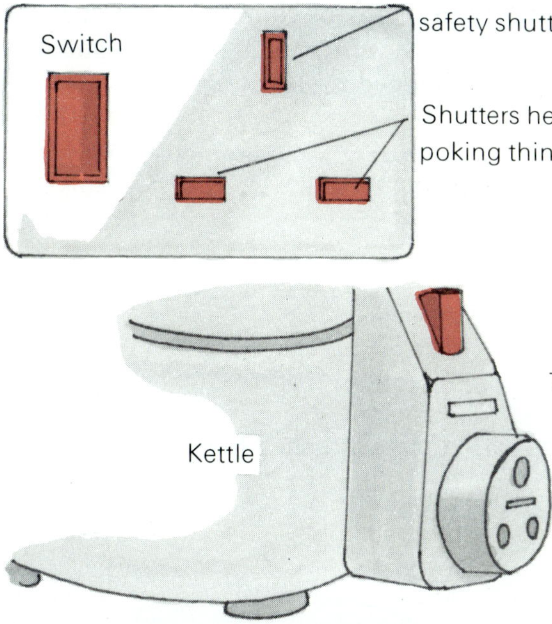

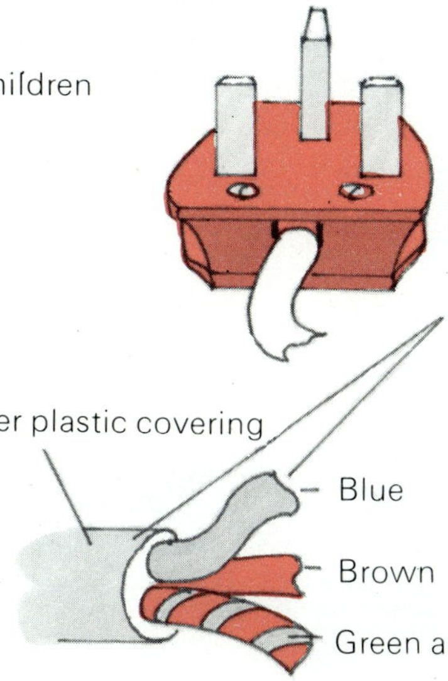

The wires inside the main flex are different colours and each colour has a very important meaning. It is important that anyone wiring a plug knows the meaning of each colour.

Each of these wires must be connected to the correct terminal inside the plug.

Here is a plug correctly wired.

Whenever a plug is wired it is essential that correct instructions are carefully followed. It is also a good safety measure to have the wiring checked against an accurate wiring diagram by someone experienced.

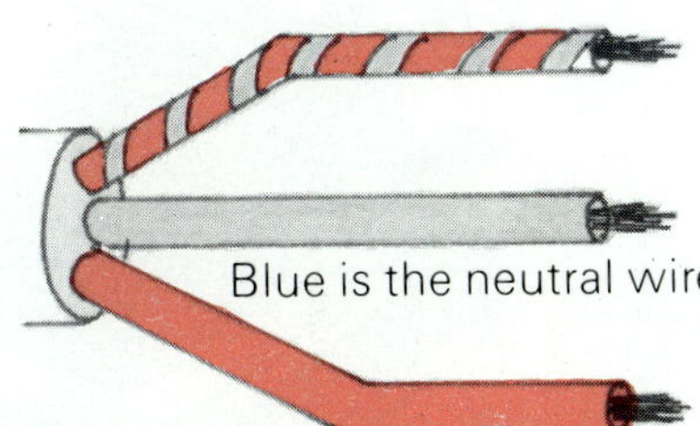

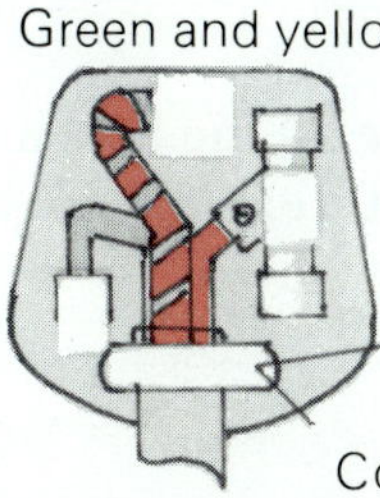

Your teacher may be able to show you the correct way to wire a plug according to the wiring diagram shown above.

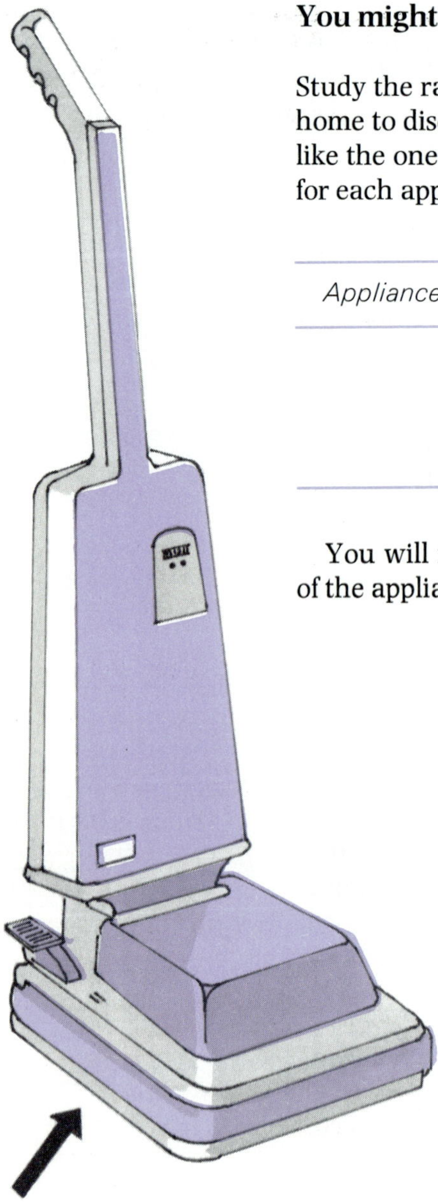

You might like to try this next part at home

Study the rating plate on the electrical equipment which you use at home to discover the power rating. Present your findings in a chart like the one shown below. Add to the chart the type of fuse suitable for each appliance you have mentioned.

Appliance	*Power rating*	*Fuse needed*

You will find the metal rating plate attached to the base or back of the appliances.

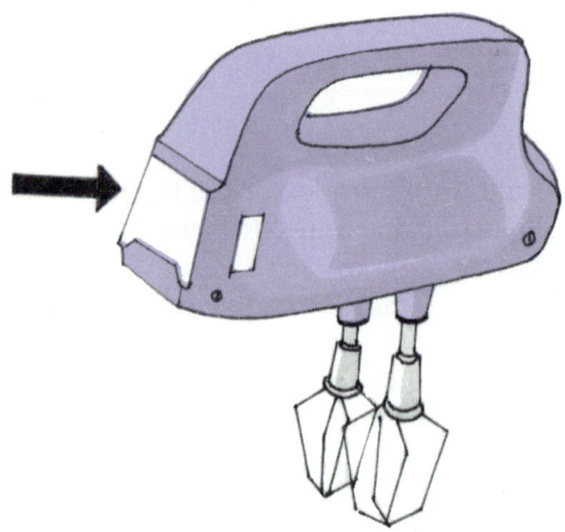

Before you begin your investigation make sure all the appliances are unplugged. It would also be a good idea to explain to your family exactly what you are doing.

USING AND PAYING FOR ELECTRICITY

Topic 9

Electricity is used in the home to supply heat, light and to power appliances. In this topic you are going to find out how the amount of electricity used in the home is calculated and paid for.

The amount of electricity used is measured in *units* and the number of units used is recorded by a special meter. Often the meter is placed under a stairway, in a hallway or sometimes in a lockable cupboard outside the house or flat. The meter is usually read every three months to find out how many units have been used. Usually a meter reader sent by the electricity board will record the units used or households may read their own meter and send in a customer reading. It is also possible to have a coin-operated meter so that electricity is paid for as it is used.

If the meter reader cannot read the meter and a customer reading is not sent then an estimated bill will be sent.

There are two kinds of meter: a digital meter; a dial meter.

A dial meter
Reading this type of meter is more complicated.

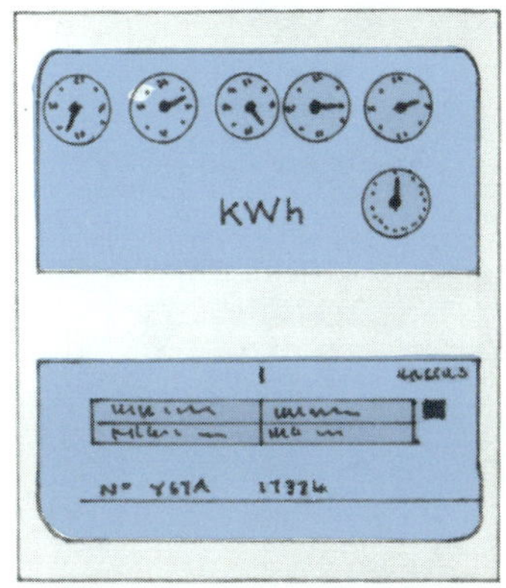

Starting from the left read the dials as shown below.

A digital meter

This is the modern type of meter.
The number of units used is shown by a row of figures.

Reading shown is

10 000 1000 100 10 1 1/10

These figures read from left to right
The meter reading is 00020

DIAL 1 Pointer has passed 4, reading is 4

DIAL 2 Pointer is directly over 5, write down 5

DIAL 3 Pointer has passed 9, reading is 9

DIAL 4 Pointer has passed 2, reading is 2

DIAL 5 Pointer is directly over 8, write down 8

10 000 1000 100 10 1 kW

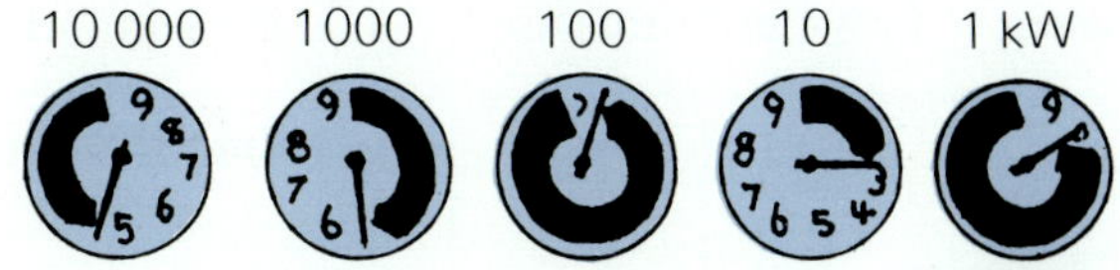

The meter reading is 45928

Ignore this dial

To find out exactly how many units have been used the present meter reading must be compared with the previous meter reading. The difference between the two is the number of units used.
For example:

Present reading –	Previous reading =	The number of units used
02581	02171	410

At the end of every quarter (3 months) householders are sent an electricity bill. On this bill the present and previous meter reading is shown along with the number of units used and the cost for each unit.

Here is an example of an electricity bill.

Meter reading		Units used	Unit price (pence)	V.A.T. code	Amount £
Present	Previous				
05464	04758	706	5.590	0	39.46
Standing charge				0	7.45
		Normal reading date		AMOUNT TO PAY	
		2 Jan 85		£46.91	

A unit of electricity costs approximately 5.5 pence.

Using a sentence answer these questions in your book.

- Your present meter reading is 84671. Your previous reading was 83250. How many units have you used and what will they cost you?
- In the last three months you have used 700 units of electricity. What will this cost you?

Work in twos. Look carefully at the meter readings shown here. Then write them down in your books adding the missing figures.

Meter readings

Present	Previous	Units used
	02581	569

Present	Previous	Units used
04336	03786	

Present	Previous	Units used
02581		410

Therefore electricity used is measured in units and each unit costs a certain amount of money. The amount for each unit is shown on the electricity bill (see the example of the bill on this page).

The amount of electricity used

The amount of electricity used depends on two things:
1 The amount of power or number of watts an appliance uses.
2 The length of time for which each appliance is used.

Table giving the usage of different appliances for 1 unit of electricity

Appliance	Watts required/ Power rating	Use for 1 unit
Toaster	800 to 950	70 slices of toast
Stereo cassette	30	8–10 hours listening
Mixer	150	60 cakes mixed
Hairdryer	500	12 ten-minute sessions
Curling tongs	20	25 half-hour sessions
Television black/white	12	9 hours viewing
Television colour	87	6 hours viewing
Kettle	2400	12 pints of boiling water
Vacuum cleaner	900	2 hours cleaning
Iron	800	2 hours use
Liquidizer	330	225 litres of soup
Fluorescent strip light	40	20 hours of light
Light bulb	100	10 hours of light
Slow cooker	50 to 150	8 hours of use

From the table above you can see that appliances with a low power rating can be used for a long time before one unit is used up.

In comparison appliances in the home such as washing machines, refrigerators and cookers have a high power rating and use more electricity.

Look at the table shown on page 34 to find out the units of electricity used during normal use of appliances with a high power rating.

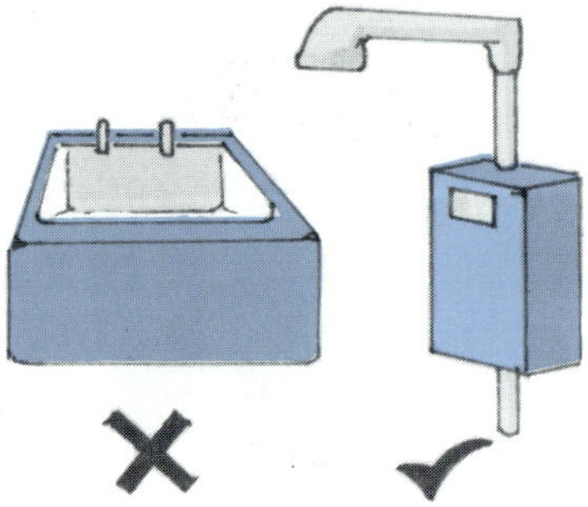

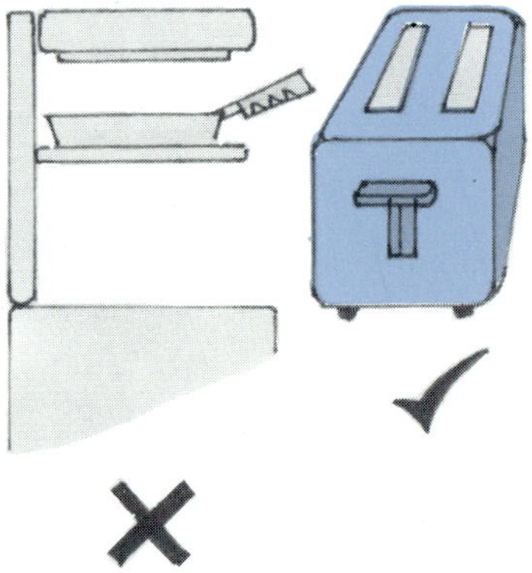

Table giving units used by different appliances in normal usage

Appliance	Normal use	Units used
Cooker	One week's meals for 4 people	20
Freezer (chest – 8 cubic feet)	Per week	12
Fridge/freezer	Per week	14
Tumble dryer	Thirty minutes drying	1
Automatic washing machine	Weekly wash for 4 people	9
Twin-tub washing machine	Weekly wash for 4 people	12
Hot-water tank well insulated	One week's hot water for 4 people	65

Make a list of the electrical appliances used in your home which you think use the most units of electricity each week. Remember that the amount of electricity used depends on the power rating of the appliance and the length of time that it is used.

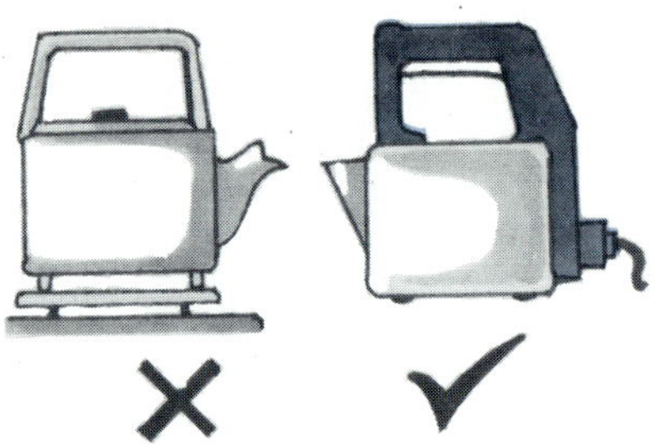

Saving electricity

The more units of electricity a household uses the more money it will have to pay. So it is important to save electricity wherever possible and not to waste it.

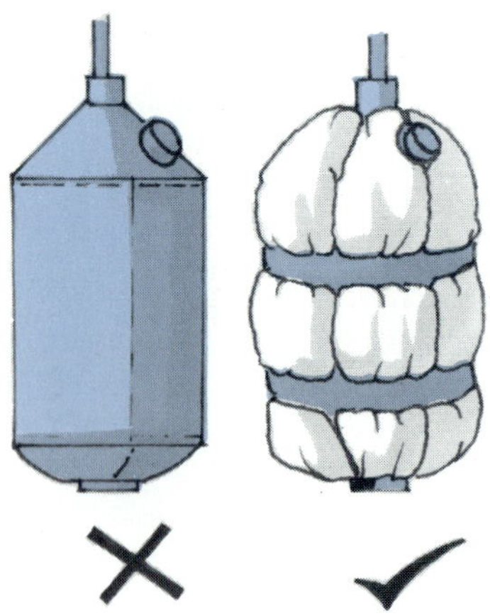

Ways in which electricity can be saved

1 Turn off lights when you are not in the room.

2 Never wash dishes under a running hot tap. Put the plug in the basin or use a bowl.

3 Fix dripping taps. They waste hot water.

4 Showers use less hot water than baths.

5 It is more economical to use a toaster than a grill.

6 Electric kettles are quicker and more economical to use for boiling water than a cooker ring. Only put in as much water as you really need when boiling a kettle though you should ensure that the element is always covered.

7 Turn off the television if you are not really watching it.

8 Hot-water tanks should be well insulated (see Topic 7).

9 Save up a full load for washing machines according to the manufacturer's instructions.

10 Make sure refrigerator and freezer doors fit properly. Open the refrigerator door as little as possible.

You might like to try this next part at home

Following the instructions given in this topic for reading a meter – calculate how many units of electricity were used in your home during one week. You should explain to your family what you are doing and ask permission before you start. You will need to draw a chart like the one shown here to record your results.

	Date	Time	Meter reading
1st reading			
2nd reading			

To calculate the units used
2nd reading – 1st reading = units used.

To calculate the cost
Total units used × unit price of 5.5 pence = Total cost of units used.

Topic 10

SAVING TIME AND WORK WITH ELECTRICITY

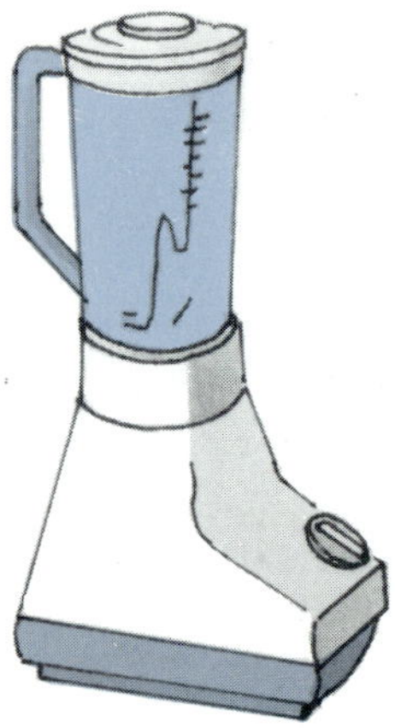

In Topic 8 you found out that electricity can be used to drive or work motors. In this topic you are going to use two kitchen appliances which have electric motors: a liquidizer; a mixer.

Liquidizers (blenders)

Liquidizers can be used to blend soups, puree fruit and vegetables, chop nuts and make breadcrumbs. Liquidizers can be bought separately or as an attachment to an electric mixer. The goblet or jug can be made from plastic or heavy glass and has a tightly fitting lid. Liquidizers should be used carefully according to the makers instructions. It is best to run the motor for short periods to prevent the motor overheating. To clean the goblet half fill it with warm water and a squeeze of detergent, put the lid on and run the motor for a few seconds. Pour out the cleaning water and rinse and dry well. Take care not to touch the blades as these are sharp. Unplug the motor and wipe clean with a damp cloth – never immerse the motor in water.

Liquidizers are economical to use – 225 litres of soup for 1 unit.

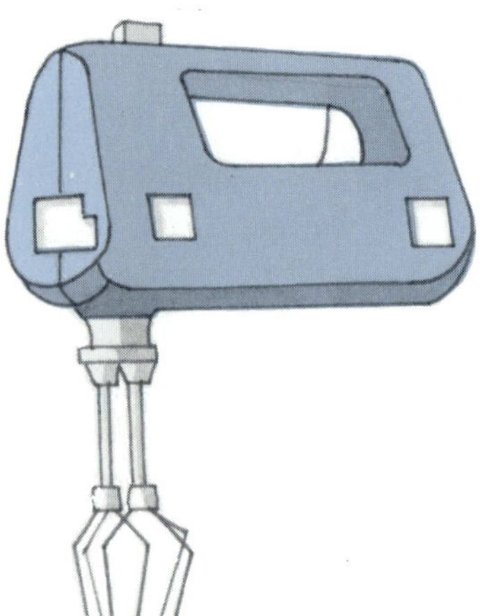

Mixers

Mixers use very little electricity – 60 cakes mixed for 1 unit. Mixers can be small hand-held models or free-standing with a mixing bowl attached. Mixers are useful for creaming cakes, rubbing fat into flour, whisking egg whites or cream. Larger free-standing models may have a dough hook and can be used for making bread. Mixers are easy to clean as the beaters can be removed for thorough washing.

Food processors

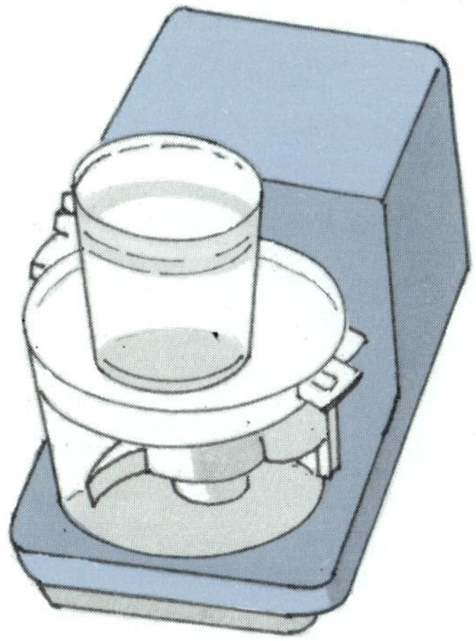

Although you will not be using a food processor in these experiments, it is useful to know what they can do.

A food processor is a machine which can do many different things. Using a food processor you can peel, chop and grate vegetables, mince meat, make breadcrumbs, puree mixtures and make pastry. In the base of the machine there is a motor which turns the attachment blades. A plastic bowl with a lid and 'chimney' covers the attachments. Food to be processed is dropped down the chimney and the machine operates with the lid firmly in position. The plastic bowl can be removed easily for cleaning.

You are going to work in twos or threes to complete one of the experiments shown here.

The experiments are designed to compare the differences in time between making up a packet cake mix by hand beating and making up a packet cake mix using an electric mixer; making up a smooth soup by hand sieving and making a smooth soup using a liquidizer.

The experiments will be shared around the class so that small groups can: complete one of the experiments;
record their results;
present and display their dish;
make comparisons and discuss their findings.

Before you begin draw a chart like the one shown below to record your results. For timing your work during the experiment you will need a watch, clock, minute timer or stop watch.

Dish made	*Equipment used for mixing or blending*	*Exact time taken for beating or blending*	*Total time including clearing away*	*Comments – appearance texture, taste*
Cake made with mixer				
Cake made by hand				
Soup – liquidized				
Soup – sieved by hand				

Experiment to compare the times taken to make up a packet cake mix using a mixer and by hand beating

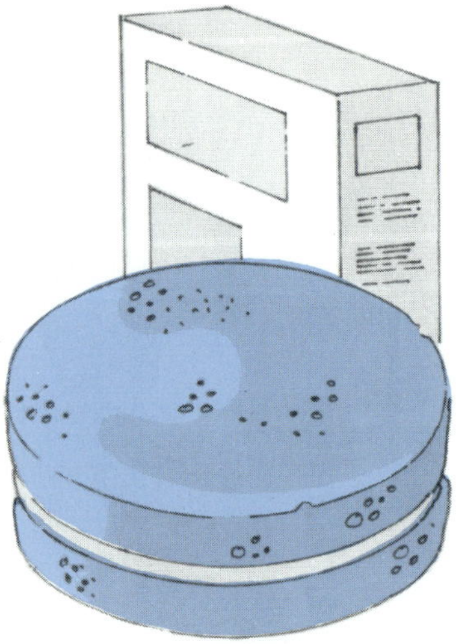

You will need

1 packet of cake mix
ingredients to make up the cake mix according to instructions on the packet
baking tins as described on the packet
1 wooden spoon or electric mixer

Method

1 Record the start time. Follow the packet instructions exactly, using either a wooden spoon or electric mixer.
2 Once you get to the stage of beating keep a careful record of the time taken.
3 Complete the packet mix according to the instructions and bake.
4 Clear away as quickly as you can and record on your results chart the total time it has taken to prepare the dish.
5 When the cake is baked sandwich together as instructed.
6 To display, cut the cake in half and place on two plates.
7 Complete the results chart.

Experiment to compare the times taken to make tangy tomato soup using a blender and by hand sieving

You will need

400 grams of canned tomatoes
a squeeze of lemon juice
a twist of freshly ground pepper
100 ml of cold water
a dash of Worcester sauce
chopped parsley or toasted bread cubes to garnish
a liquidizer or a sieve and wooden spoon

Method

Using a liquidizer

1 Record the start time.
2 Place the goblet in position.
3 Pour the tomatoes and the juice into the goblet and add the other ingredients.
4 Put the lid on the goblet and turn on the motor for two or three short bursts or until the mixture is smooth. Time this stage carefully and record it.
5 Pour the tomato mixture into a saucepan and heat gently.
6 To serve, pour into soup bowls and garnish with parsley or toasted bread cubes.
7 Clear away and record the total time taken on your results chart.

Using a sieve and wooden spoon

1 Record the start time.
2 Position the sieve over a mixing bowl and pour in half the tomatoes.
3 Time this stage carefully. Use the back of the wooden spoon to press the tomatoes through the holes in the sieve.
4 Repeat until all the tomatoes are finely sieved. Add the other ingredients and mix well.
5 Pour the tomato mixture into a saucepan and heat gently.
6 To serve, pour into soup bowls and garnish with parsley or toasted bread cubes.
7 Clear away and record the total time taken on your results chart.

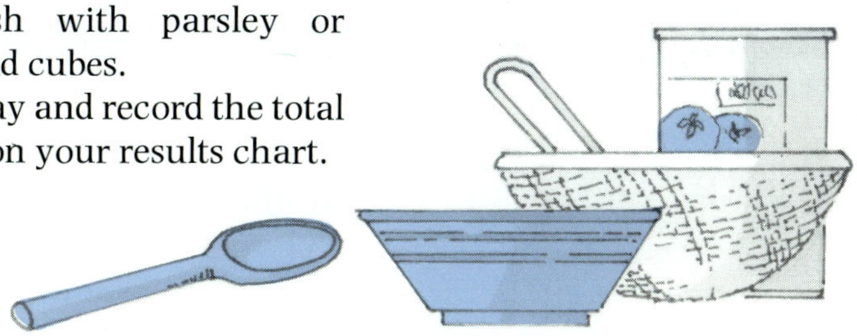

Displaying and making comparisons

Each group should make a label for the dish that they have made. An example is given in the margin.

Dish – packet cake mix
Equipment – electric mixer
Total time –
Beating time –

On a large table display all the labelled dishes. With the teacher and the rest of the class discuss the results of each experiment – in particular the total time taken and the beating or blending time.

Tasting

Each dish should be tasted using separate spoons and dishes for each person. Take a sip of water in between each tasting to cleanse your palate.

Conclusion

Complete the results chart using the information on the display labels and from the findings of your tasting.

You might like to try this next part at home

Conduct a survey to find out the prices of liquidizers and mixers on sale.

Record your findings in a chart.

Appliance description	*Power rating*	*Price*

Then write a sentence or two to say which mixer and which liquidizer you would advise people to buy and why.

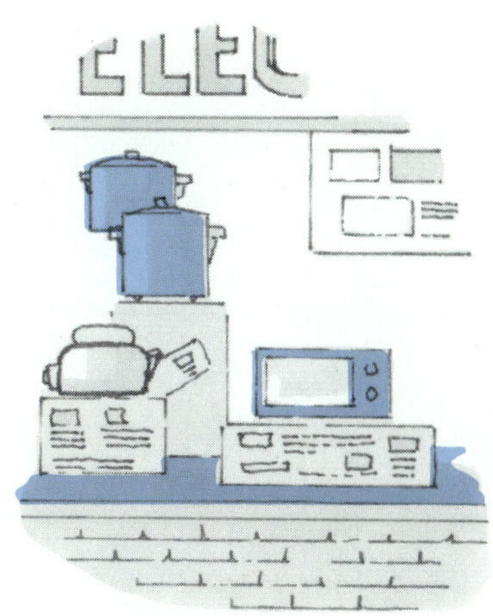

Topic 11 TECHNOLOGY AND FOOD

In this topic you are going to find out about the influence of technology on foods that you eat. Just one look at the picture of a supermarket shows you that very few of the foods eaten regularly are untouched by technology. Only fresh fruit, vegetables, meat, eggs and fish are largely unprocessed and even these will have been produced in a special way.
For example: fertilizers are added to soil to encourage plants to grow; animals are fed special diets to ensure lean meat.

Almost any food we can think of has been processed and partly or totally prepared in some way by manufacturers. Easy to prepare and ready-to-eat foods are very convenient – making cooking and meal planning a fast and easy task.

Food technology is big business and every day new developments in the food industry produce new varieties and types of prepared foods.

Almost every home's food cupboard will contain a range of these convenience foods. In fact these foods are very popular and here are some of the reasons why:

1 people can save time by using convenience foods;

2 greater advances in food technology mean that there is more variety;

3 more households have freezers and can store frozen convenience foods;
4 convenience foods are advertised regularly on television and in magazines;
5 prices of these foods are relatively low because of competition between manufacturers.

Here are some diagrams showing the types of convenience foods sold. They have been grouped according to the way they have been processed.

Draw the diagrams into your book and for each of the groups write down examples of convenience foods that you eat regularly.

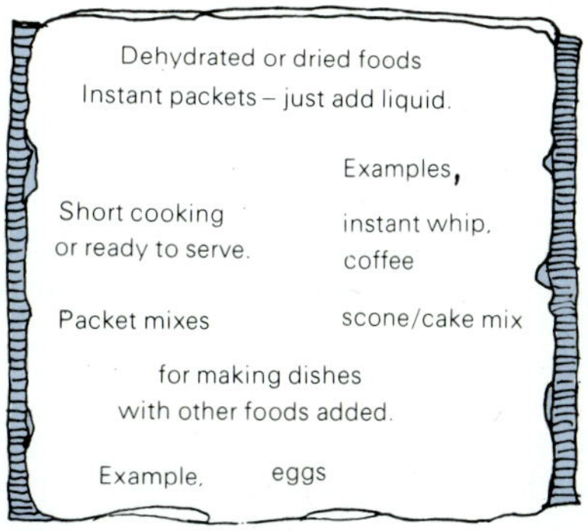

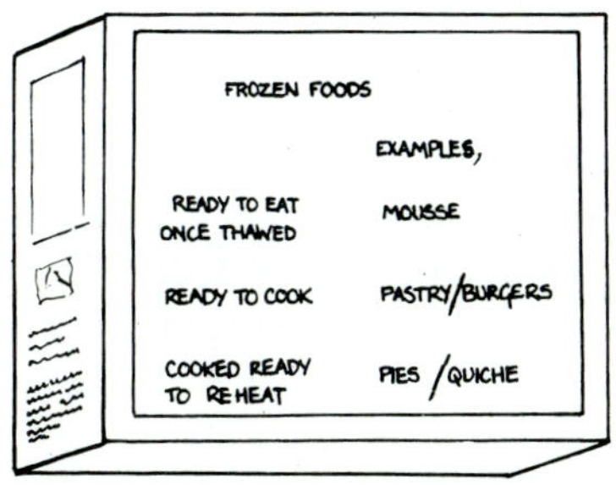

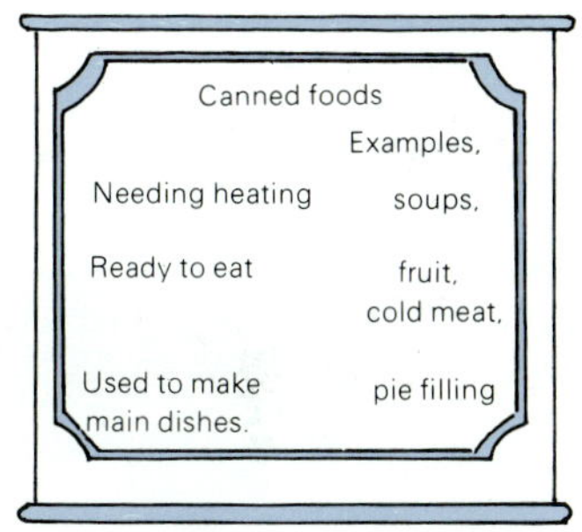

Texturized vegetable protein

The dried convenience foods shown in the margin are savoury products which contain a meat substitute made from soya beans and called texturized vegetable protein (TVP). Plant seeds, like peas, beans and cereals are a good source of protein. Manufacturers use a special process to turn the protein of soya beans into a product which looks like meat. The soya protein (which is flavourless) is then flavoured and used in recipes instead of meat or added to small amounts of meat to make them go further.

The advantages of using TVP

1 It is cheaper than meat.
2 People who do not like or do not want to eat meat can eat TVP instead.
3 TVP has no flavour of its own so can be added to meat, fish or fruit mixtures to make them go further.

With the help of your teacher, work as a class to conduct an experiment to evaluate the colour, texture, taste and appearance of Spaghetti Bolognese sauce made with: TVP packet mix; minced meat; TVP and meat.

Working in small groups you will need to divide these tasks around the class.

1 Prepare sample dishes of Spaghetti Bolognese sauce using:
a TVP packet mix and following the packet instructions;
minced meat made up to the recipe shown below;
50% minced meat and 50% TVP packet mix.

Follow the recipe shown and add the TVP along with the liquid. The combined mixture can then be cooked together according to the recipe.

Recipe

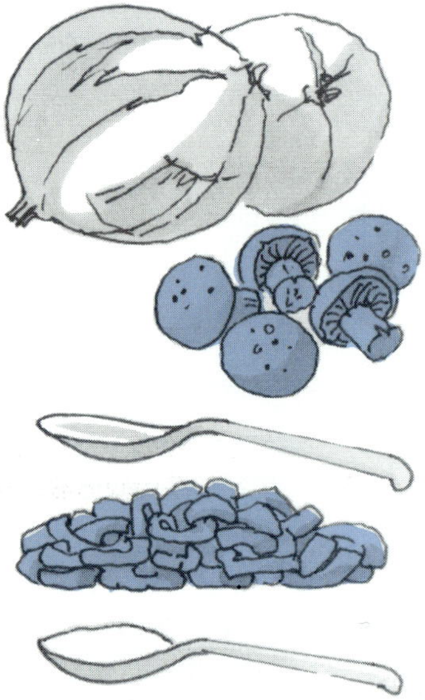

Spaghetti Bolognese sauce

Ingredients

1 onion
100 grams mushrooms
1 level tablespoon of cooking oil
200 grams minced beef
1 rounded tablespoon flour
1 large can tomatoes
100 ml of water
1 stock cube
freshly ground black pepper to taste

Method

1 Peel and chop the onion. Wash and slice the mushrooms.
2 Heat the oil in a pan and lightly sauté the onions and mushrooms.
3 Add the minced meat and stir gently until brown all over.
4 Stir in the flour. Add the tomatoes, water, stock cube and pepper.
5 Bring to the boil, then simmer gently for 20 to 30 minutes with the lid on. Remember to stir occasionally.

2 Keep a record of the preparation and cooking time.
3 Work out the total cost of each dish.
4 Prepare labels ready to display with each dish. Use numbers or letters on the labels so that tasters can make up their own minds.
5 Have ready a glass of water, a small plate and a spoon for each taster.

Each person will need to draw in their books both a results and a rating chart, as shown on page 43, to record the results of the experiment and the tasting.

Results chart

Spaghetti Bolognese sauce	Total cost of dish	Time to prepare	Time to cook	Appearance – colour, shape	Taste and texture – salty, spicy, sugary, chewy, crunchy, smooth
TVP mix					
Meat recipe					
Meat and TVP recipe					

Rating chart

List each dish and give it a mark out of five (5 = highest; 1 = lowest).

Sauce	Convenience	Taste	Value for money

You might like to try this next part at home

Conduct your own survey to assess the number of television advertisements relating to convenience foods. You should watch the television for selected periods of about 15 to 20 minutes at peak viewing times in the late afternoon and evening.

Draw a chart like the one below to record your observations.

Time of viewing	Convenience food advertised – describe	What is the selling point of the advertisement? E.g. convenience, taste, cost

Topic 12 ADDITIVES IN FOOD

Ingredients:
Mandarin orange segments, Water, Sugar

Labels on most prepacked foods must include a complete list of ingredients. If you look at the label on any convenience food you will find an ingredients list which shows in descending order of weight exactly what went into the food.
For example: A can of mandarin oranges has this ingredients list showing that mandarin orange segments make up most of the net weight (See Topic 13 in Book 1).

Added water must be included in the list if it makes up more than 5% of the net weight and any food additives must also be listed. Manufacturers are allowed to add safe and tested substances to food for the following reasons: to preserve them from decay and spoilage; to improve flavour, colour and texture; to improve the keeping qualities; to produce an identical product every time in large scale manufacture; to provide a wide range of convenience foods for the consumer.

Additives such as sugar, salt, spices and alcohol are examples of preservatives which have been added to foods for centuries. Additives are usually listed by their category names which explain the main function they perform in the food and these names are usually followed by the additives' chemical names or serial 'E' numbers. For example: an ingredients list from a packet of potato rings as shown below.

INGREDIENTS : DRIED POTATO, VEGETABLE OIL, STARCH, SALT, EMULSIFIER (E471), FLAVOUR ENHANCER,(MONOSODIUM GLUTAMATE), ANTIOXIDANTS,(E320,E321)

Emulsifier E471

Antioxidant E320 and E321

What are 'E' numbers?

You will have noticed that the letter 'E' in front of a series of numbers appears on many ingredients lists. In order that foods can be moved from country to country within the Common Market, a list of additives that have been tested and recognized as safe have been introduced. These additives have been given a special 'E' number. Since the 1st January 1986, all foods (except for flavourings) must have the 'E' number or the actual name of the additive listed with the ingredients. Many additives have very long names and there would not be room to list them all on some packets so the 'E' numbers are a useful code.

Knowing the meaning of the 'E' numbers

Make sure you know what the 'E' numbers mean by looking at the table shown here to find out about: the types of additives; their main function in foods; their 'E' number category.

Type of additive	Function in food	'E' number category
Permitted colours	Colours are added to make foods look more attractive. Some colours are natural substances such as, saffron, chlorophyll and paprika. No colours are allowed to be added to fresh meats, fish, poultry, vegetables or fruits although colours can be used for marking. No colours are allowed to be added to condensed or dried milk, tea or coffee.	E100 to E180 E.g. E102 is a commonly used colouring. Added to many packet foods such as sweets, fruit squashes, fizzy drinks, salad cream, pre-packed cakes.
Preservatives	Slow down or prevent the growth of micro-organisms in foods. The use of these preservatives ensures that a variety of foods is available all the year round.	E200 to E290 E.g. E200 is added to yoghurt, sweets, soft drinks, processed cheese, frozen pizza.
Antioxidants	Many food products are badly affected by oxygen in the air. For example oils and fats can go rancid. Antioxidants, some of which are natural (vitamins C and E) are added to foods to stop them being spoiled by oxygen.	E300 to E321 E.g. E320 and E321 are added to biscuits, sweets, soft drinks, cheese spread, savoury rice, potato rings and chewing gum.
Emulsifiers and stabilizers	Emulsifiers are added to foods to ensure that oils and fats mix in with water and other ingredients to make a smooth and stable mixture. Stabilizers stop oils and water from separating out during storage. Some emulsifiers are natural products like E322 found in eggs.	E322 to E494 E.g. E322 is added to, packet trifle mix, yoghurt whip and chocolate biscuits. E450 is added to cold meats and frozen poultry to tenderize. This also can be a way of adding water to foods.
Permitted sweeteners	Added to help stop deposits of crystals forming in sucrose syrups.	E420 and E421.
Flavour enhancer – Monosodium glutamate (MSG)	Improves the flavour of foods. It occurs naturally in a type of Japanese seaweed but is usually commercially prepared from wheat gluten and sugar beet.	Has no 'E' number yet. MSG is added to packet snacks, soups, pork pies and sausages. Too much MSG can be dangerous.

Emulsifier - to keep oil and water mixed together

So with this information it is possible to analyse the ingredients lists on the foods that we eat, to find out about the additives they contain. For example: analysing an ingredients label from wholemeal bread.

Work in twos to analyse the ingredients labels on different convenience foods, such as: packet cake mixes; soups; sauces; desserts; potato snacks; tinned main meals; stews; sauces; soups; puddings and custard; sausages; cold meats; meat pies; fish fingers; fish cakes etc.

Before you begin draw a chart like the one below. An example has been started for you.

Product – Potato rings		
List of ingredients in descending order of weight	*Description of each ingredient (use the 'E' number chart to help you)*	*Function of the additives in the food*
Dried potato	*The main ingredient*	
Vegetable oil		
Starch		
Salt	*Added for flavour*	
E471	*Emulsifier*	
MSG	*Flavour enhancer*	
E320	*Antioxidant*	

Draw and complete a chart in your books for each of the ingredients lists that you analyse.

When you have completed three or four charts you might like to discuss your findings with your teacher and the rest of your class.

Additives and health

All the 'E' numbers have been tested and can be safely added to foods. However, many people believe that too many additives are bad for us, in the same way as an excess of sugar and salt. Some people particularly children are sensitive to food additives. It is hard to totally avoid eating food additives, however we can read labels to ensure that we do not eat regularly products which contain lots of food additives. From the analysing you have done in this topic you should have a good idea of which foods contain the most additives.

You might like to try this next part at home

Collect the labels or make a note of the ingredients listed on the foods which you eat during the week, particularly sweets, snacks and fizzy drinks.

Make a list of the 'E' numbers contained in these foods and their functions.

Write down the 'E' numbers which occur most often.

If you want to avoid eating too many food additives which foods should you cut out of your diet?

Topic 13 COOKING VEGETABLES

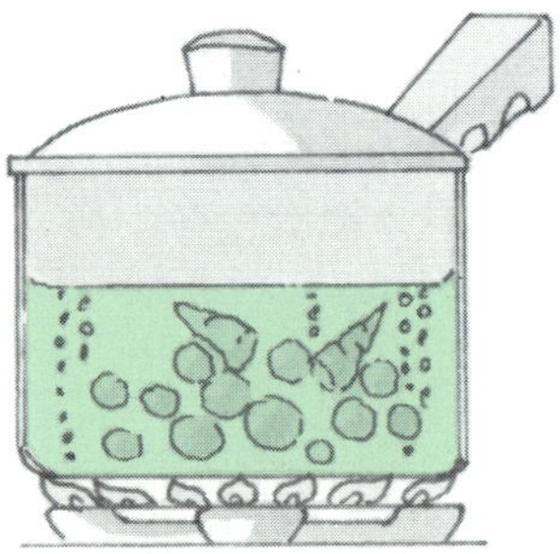

Vegetables are an important food resource because they contain important vitamins and minerals and also because they add colour and variety to the diet. Many vegetables can be eaten raw. In this state they have a firm and crunchy texture and contain nearly all of their vitamins and minerals. Vegetables can also be cooked. This softens them, makes them easier to eat and digest and adds variety to mealtimes. However cooking does destroy the water-soluble vitamins in the vegetable – especially vitamin C. To prevent huge losses of vitamin C during cooking it is important that vegetables are cooked for as little time as possible in a small amount of water in a covered saucepan. Never add bicarbonate of soda (an alkali) to the cooking liquid. It will give the vegetables a green colour but it will also destroy vitamin C and make the vegetables mushy! The cooking liquid should also be used whenever possible in sauces, stocks and gravy.

Make a list in your books of the names of vegetables you regularly eat both raw and cooked. An example has been given for you.

Vegetable	*Raw*	*Cooked*
Tomato	*In sandwiches*	*Grilled*

The colour of vegetables

The vegetables shown in the picture below are green in colour. This is because they contain a green pigment called chlorophyll.

Chlorophyll is sensitive to pH or acid or alkali conditions (see Topic 5).

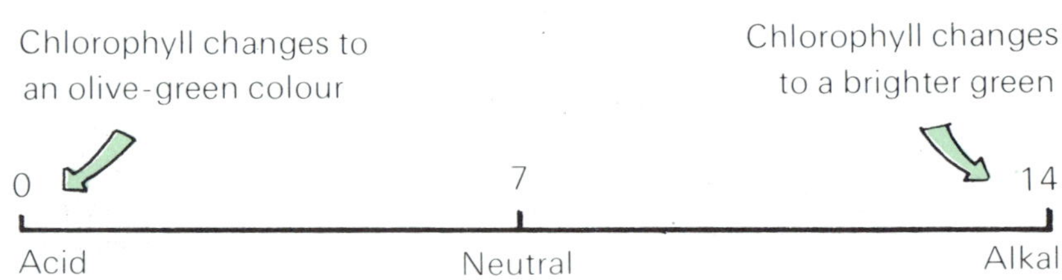

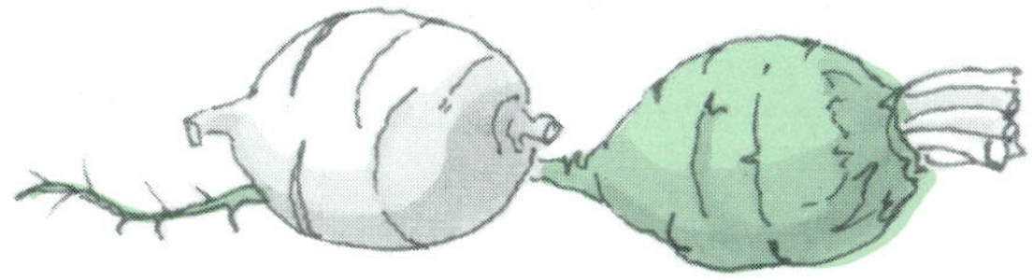

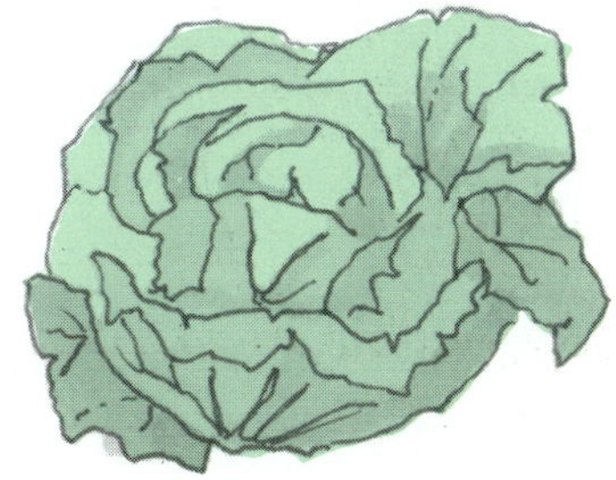

The vegetables shown above are a deep red colour, because they contain pigments called anthocyanins. These are also sensitive to pH.

They are red — Anthocyanins in vegetables, e.g. red cabbage, are bright red — They are blue

Acid 0 —— Neutral 7 —— Alkali 14

Work as a class to complete the experiment shown here. Work in groups of two so that each group carries out one part of the experiment. The results of each part of the experiment will be displayed for everyone to see, taste and discuss, when each group has finished.

Experiment to find out the effect of pH on the colour, texture and flavour of cooked green and red cabbage

Each group will need
500 ml boiling water
1 medium saucepan with a lid
1 draining spoon
1 saucer
1 measuring jug
pH indicator paper and a colour chart
paper to make two labels

Groups 1 to 4 will use green cabbage and the ingredients listed below.
Groups 5 to 8 will complete the same experiments as groups 1 to 4 but will use red cabbage instead of green.

Groups 1 and 5 – 50 grams shredded cabbage + 2 level tablespoons vinegar.
Groups 2 and 6 – 50 grams shredded cabbage + 1 level teaspoon salt.
Groups 3 and 7 – 50 grams shredded cabbage + nothing else.
Groups 4 and 8 – 50 grams shredded cabbage + $\frac{1}{2}$ teaspoon bicarbonate of soda.
*Teacher – Put 50 grams of each type of cabbage on two separate saucers and label. These samples are the controls.

Before you begin draw in your books a results chart like the one shown on the next page.

Group	Cabbage sample	Cooked with	pH of liquid	Colour of liquid	Colour of cabbage	Texture	Flavour
1							
2							
3							
4							
5							
6							
7							
8							
Red control							
Green control							

Group 1	Green cabbage +vinegar Cooking liquid
pH =	

Group 1: Cabbage sample cooked with vinegar in water

Method

1 Put the water in a saucepan. Add the vinegar, salt or bicarbonate of soda and the cabbage.

2 Put a lid on the pan and cook over a medium heat for 5 minutes.

3 Remove the pan from the heat. Use a draining spoon to lift the cooked cabbage out of the cooking liquid and place on the saucer.

4 Pour the cooking liquid into a measuring jug and leave to cool. Make a label for the saucer and the jug, as shown in the margin.

5 Take an indicator paper and dip one end into the cooking liquid. Carefully check the colour of the paper against the colour chart. Decide on the pH of the liquid and write this result in the chart and on the two labels.

6 On a large table display the labelled results of all the experiments.

Green cabbage

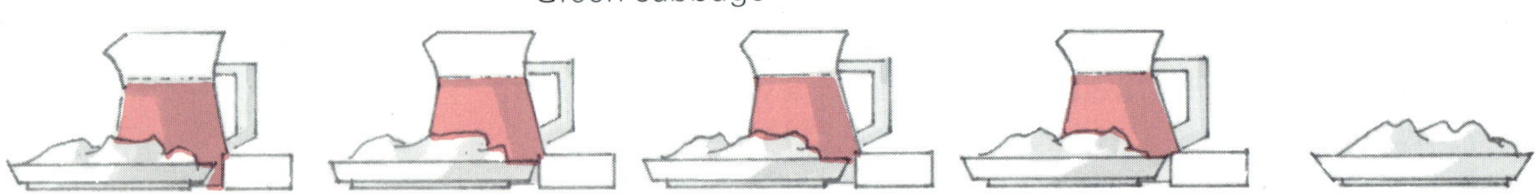

Red cabbage

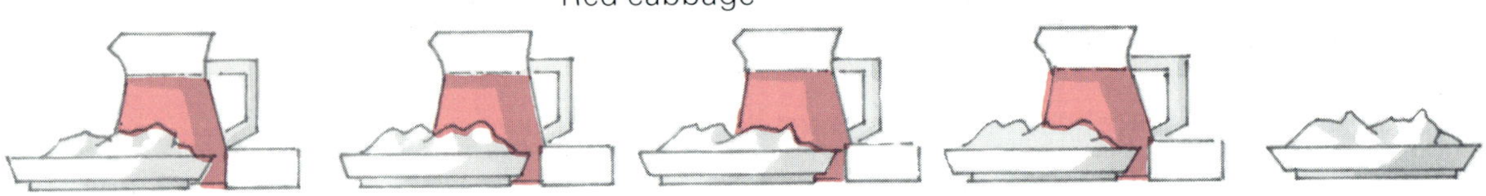

7 Look carefully at each cooked cabbage sample and the cooking liquid. Discuss with the teacher and the rest of the class what you can see, feel and taste.

8 Complete each part of the results chart using the findings of your observations and the information on the display labels.

You might like to try this next part at home

Write a paragraph to explain how you would cook green leafy vegetables to: preserve vitamin C; keep a good colour; ensure a firm texture.

Use the results of the class experiment to explain and support your answer.

Topic 14

SCIENCE AND FOOD – USING YEAST IN BREADMAKING

Yeast single cell

Bud forming

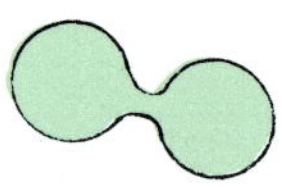

Cell begins to divide

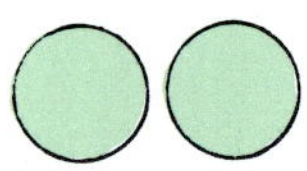

Two single yeast cells

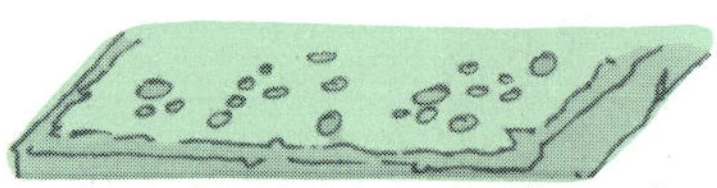

If you look closely at a slice of risen or leavened bread you can see the gas bubbles formed by yeast The gas bubbles can make large and small holes

Fresh yeast

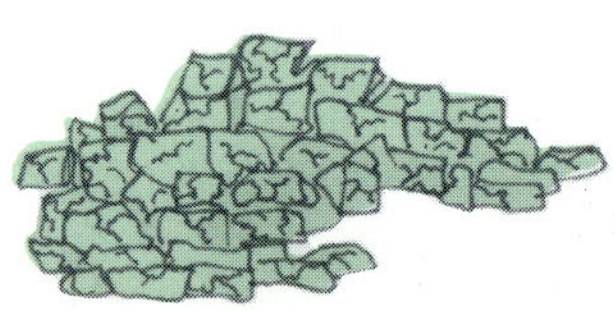

Dried yeast

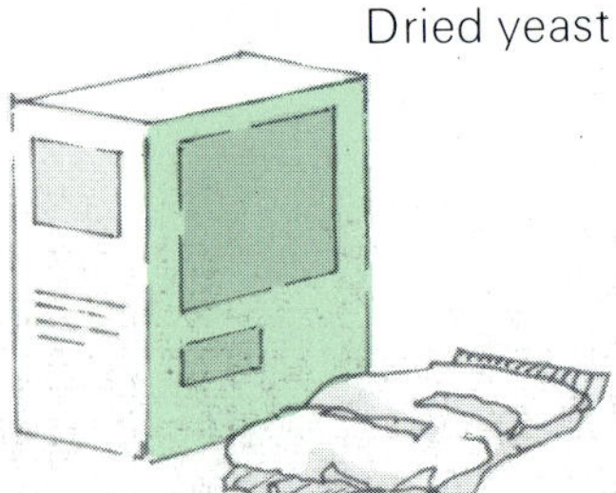

Yeasts are tiny single-celled plants which are found on the surface of fruits, in air and in soil.

Yeast cells reproduce by budding and under a microscope a yeast cell would look like the picture in the margin.

Yeast only grows if it is warm and has a supply of food and water. Very hot temperatures will kill yeast and cold temperatures slow down its growth.

As yeast cells reproduce they give off a gas called carbon dioxide (CO_2) and alcohol. When yeast is used to make bread the bubbles of the carbon dioxide given off are trapped in the dough. These gas bubbles expand in a hot oven to make open-textured and well-risen bread.

The type of yeast used in breadmaking is commercially produced. Firstly there is fresh yeast, which is a soft and creamy coloured mixture rather like putty. Also there is dried yeast, which looks like tiny pale brown grains.

Under the right conditions – when it is warm, wet and has food – these types of yeast will produce the carbon dioxide needed to make risen or leavened bread.

Work as a class to complete these experiments to find out more about yeast and the conditions it needs to work.

Divide into small groups (two or three) so that each group completes one of the six experiments shown here. The results of each experiment will be discussed when all the groups have finished.

Experiment 1

1 Mix 5 grams of fresh yeast with 50 ml of tepid (just warm) water.
2 Add this water to 100 grams of breadmaking flour and mix well into a dough.
3 Form the dough into a ball.
4 Knead the dough well on a floured board for 4 to 5 minutes.
5 Put the dough on a greased baking sheet. Cover with an oiled polythene bag and leave in a warm place for at least 15 minutes.
6 Remove the polythene bag and bake the dough on the top shelf of an oven, gas mark 8, 230 centigrade for about 15 minutes.

Experiment 2

Follow the same instructions as in Experiment 1 to make and bake a dough but *do not* use any yeast.

Experiment 3

Follow the same instructions as Experiment 1 to make a dough using yeast. When the dough has been kneaded, divide it into two and form each piece into a ball.

Put one ball of dough on a baking sheet and bake straight away at gas mark 8, 230 centigrade for 15 minutes.

Follow instructions 5 to 6 of Experiment 1 for the other ball of dough.

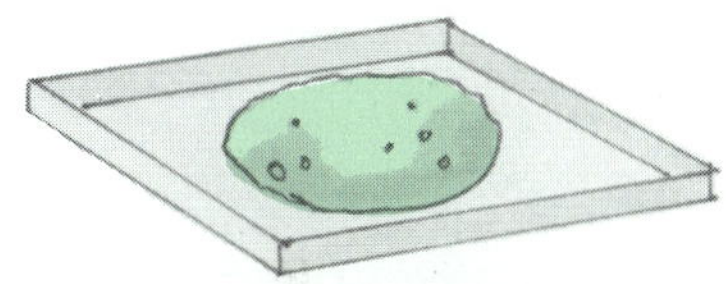

Experiment 4

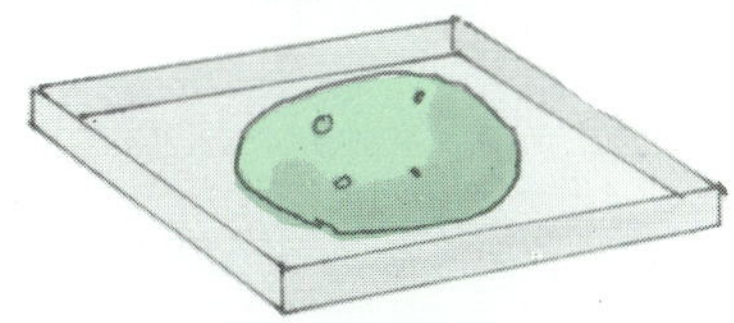

1 Follow instructions 1 to 4 of Experiment 1.
2 Then divide the dough into two and form into two balls.
3 For one of the balls follow instructions 5 to 6 of Experiment 1.
4 Place the other ball on a greased baking sheet, cover with an oiled polythene bag and place on the top shelf of a refrigerator for 15 minutes. Then remove the polythene and bake as in Experiment 1.

Experiment 5

Follow exactly the same instructions as Experiment 1 using dried yeast instead of fresh.

Experiment 6

1 Mix 5 grams of dried yeast with 50 ml of tepid (just warm) water in a beaker. Add $\frac{1}{4}$ teaspoon of sugar and mix well. Leave in a warm place for 25 minutes. Label this beaker – A.
2 Follow the instructions as in 1, but this time use freezing cold water. Label this beaker – B.
3 Follow the instructions as in 1, but this time use recently boiled, very hot water. Label this beaker – C.

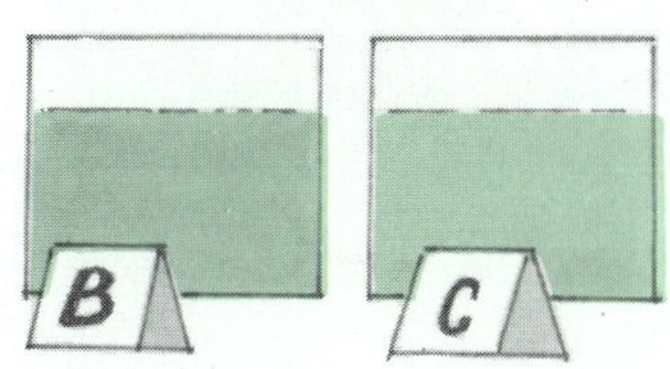

Each person should now draw a results chart like the one shown on page 54.

Experiment	*Description of the results*	*What this result tells me about yeast and the conditions it needs to work*
1 Dough with fresh yeast, risen, baked		
2 Dough with no fresh yeast, risen, baked		
3 Dough with fresh yeast, risen, baked		
Dough with fresh yeast baked straight away		
4 Dough with fresh yeast, risen in a warm place, baked		
Dough with fresh yeast, left in refrigerator, baked		
5 Dough with dried yeast, risen, baked		
6 A yeast + warm water		
B yeast + very cold water		
C yeast + very hot water		

E.g. Experiment 1

Each group will need to make labels to display the results of their experiment.

On a large table display the labelled results of each experiment. Look carefully at the results of each experiment and discuss what you can see with the rest of the class and the teacher.

Complete the results chart in your book.

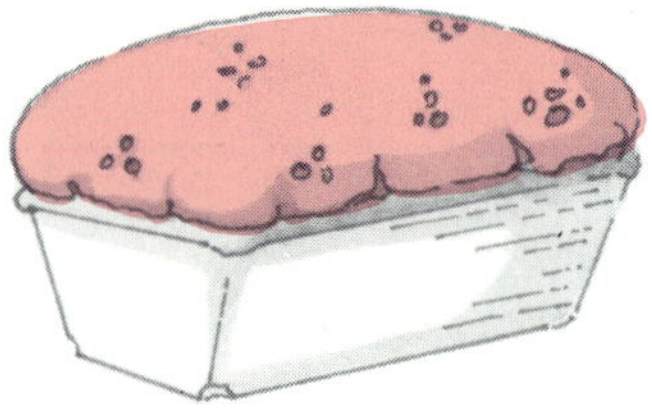

You might like to try this next part at home

Imagine that you were making bread using yeast.

Write a paragraph to explain the method you would use to: prepare the yeast; make the dough; rise it; bake it.

SCIENCE AND FOOD - MAKING BREAD FROM FLOUR

Topic 15

Different types of cereals are grown all over the world. They are an important food resource.

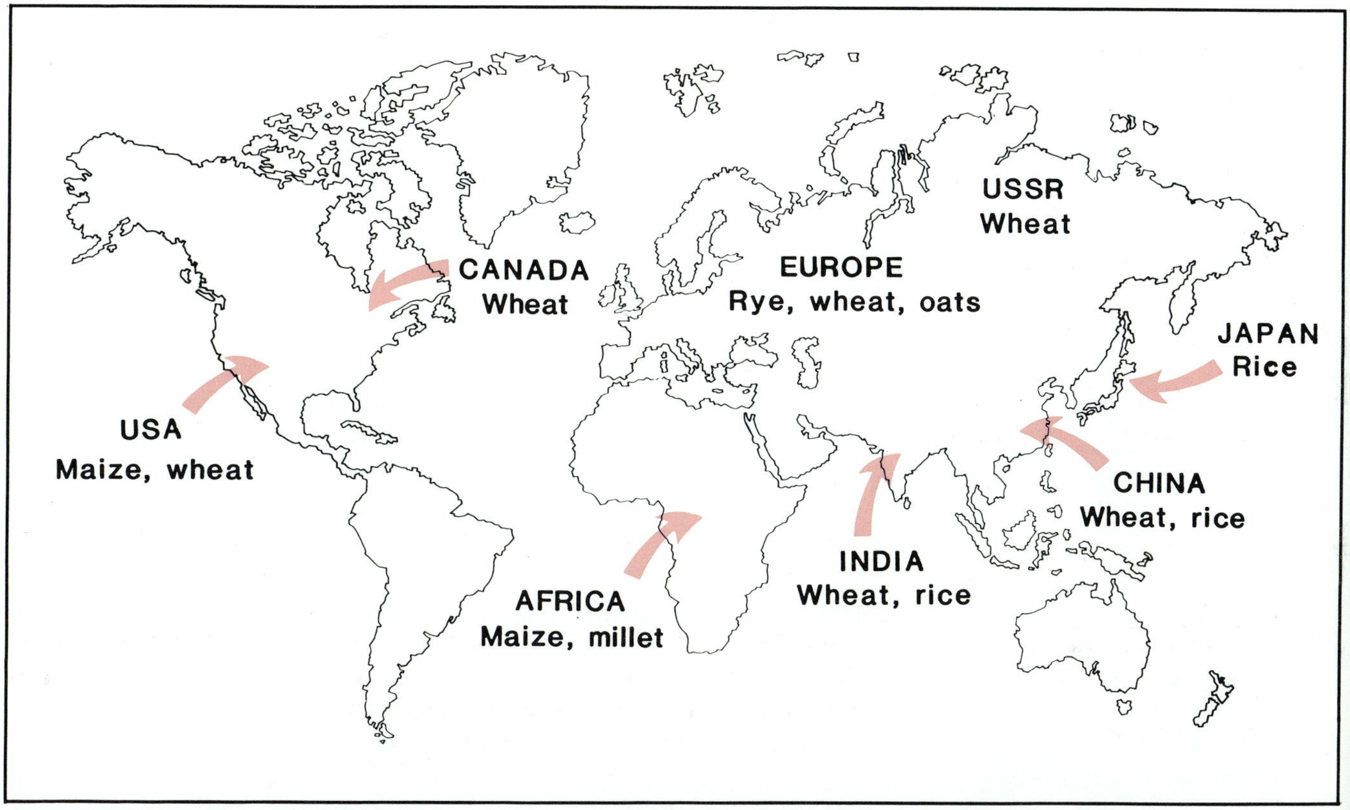

Cereals can be ground into flours.

Each flour has different properties and these decide the types of bread that it can be made into. Some flours can be made into leavened or raised breads using yeast whilst other flours can only be made into flat or unleavened breads.

Wheat flour is very versatile and is used all over the world to make many types of bread both leavened and unleavened.

The best types of wheat flour for breadmaking are strong flours. These contain a lot of *gluten* which helps to make an elastic and stretchy bread dough.

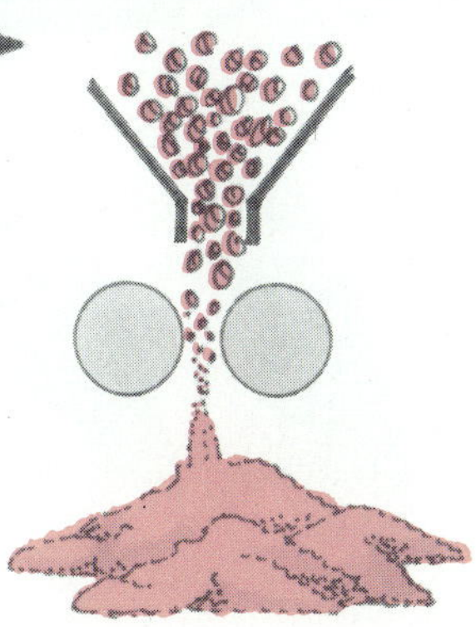

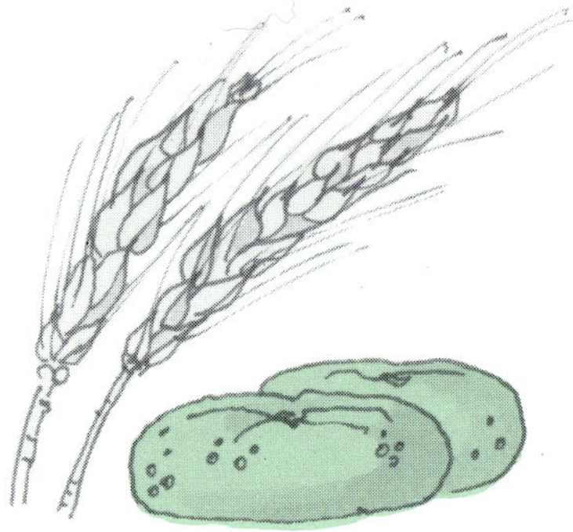

Flour	Country	Types of bread: Leavened	Types of bread: Unleavened
Rye	Germany Scandinavia	Fermented bread	Crispbread
Oats	Scotland		Oatcakes
Pulses	India		Dosas
Rice	Philippines		Puto
Maize	Mexico		Tortillas
Wheat	Ireland Middle East France India China England Italian	Soda bread Pitta bread Baton/stick croissant Man t'ou/ steamed buns Cottage loaf Coburg Pizza base Bread sticks	 Chapattis Nan

Strong wheat is grown mostly in Canada. Wheat grown in other parts of the world produces weak flour containing much less gluten. Weak flours are best for biscuit and cake making.

Work in twos for the following experiment.

Experiment to find out the amount of gluten in different types of flour

You will need

50 grams of – cornflour
– rice flour
– strong bread flour (white)
– weak cake making flour (white)

4 basins half-full with water
4 squares of muslin, 20 cms × 20 cms
String
Iodine and a dropper

Method

1 Draw a chart like the one shown here to record your results.

Type of flour	*What was left in the bag?*	*Does the liquid contain starch?* ✓	*How much gluten the flour contained*

2 Tie up each type of flour in a muslin bag.

3 Place each muslin bag in a basin of water and work the bag with the fingers to make sure all the flour has been thoroughly wetted. Do this for several minutes.

4 Hold the bag under a running cold tap until the water runs clear. Squeeze out the water from each bag.

5 Untie each bag and open it up to see what is left inside. If a flour contains gluten, an elastic substance rather like chewing-gum will be left in the bag. Roll this gummy substance into a ball and weigh it. Any starch in the flour will have been washed out into the water in the basin, which will become a milky white colour.

6 Add a drop of iodine to the water in the basin. This is a test for starch – if the colour changes to blue-black, starch is present.

7 Look carefully at the contents of each bag and at the water in each basin. Discuss with your partner what you can see.

8 Complete the results chart. You can then discuss your results with the rest of the class and the teacher.

When leavened bread is made the gluten in flour helps to form an elastic and stretchy dough which will hold the bubbles of carbon dioxide (CO_2).

What happens while bread is baking?

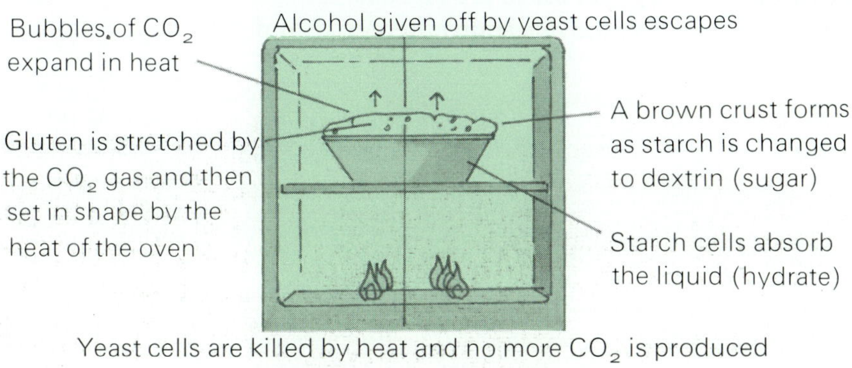

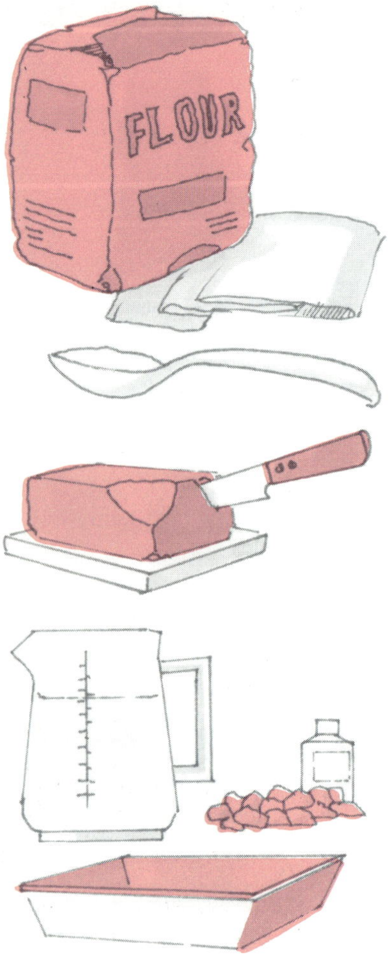

Recipe

Bread rolls using strong flour

Ingredients

250 grams strong flour, white or wholemeal
1 level teaspooon of salt
15 grams margarine
15 grams fresh yeast
125 ml water
1 × 25 mg ascorbic acid tablet (vitamin C improves the dough and shortens the making time)

Oven temperature Gas 8, 230 centigrade

You will need

1 greased 20 cm sandwich tin

Method

1 Put the flour into a bowl. Add the salt and rub in the margarine.

2 Crush the ascorbic acid tablet between two teaspoons. Put the powder into a measuring jug. Add 3 tablespoons of boiling water to dissolve the tablet.

3 Add enough cold water to the measuring jug to make 125 ml. Add the yeast to this lukewarm water and mix well.

4 Pour the water into the flour mixture and mix well to make a soft dough. Form the dough into a ball.

5 On a floured board knead the dough for about 10 minutes.

6 Cut the dough into 8 even-sized pieces – weigh each one to make sure they are the same size.

7 Form each weighed piece of dough into a ball and place in the greased sandwich tin leaving a space between each roll. Leave to rise in a warm place until nearly double in size.

8 Bake for 15 to 20 minutes until they are a light brown colour and sound hollow when tapped on the bottom.

You might like to try this next part at home

Make a survey of local shops and supermarkets to find out how many different types of bread are on sale.

Draw a chart like the one shown here to record your observations.

Type of bread, e.g. pitta	*Type of flour used, e.g. rye*	*Is it leavened or unleavened?*	*Have I tasted this bread before?*

SCIENCE AND FOOD - FOOD AND FREEZING

Topic 16

Foods are not always eaten as soon as they are harvested, prepared or slaughtered. Foods that are not eaten immediately have to be carefully packed and stored to keep them fresh.

Foods become spoiled for a number of reasons.

Firstly, most foods contain a certain amount of water. The longer that these foods are stored and exposed to air the more water they will lose due to evaporation. Water loss from foods can be slowed down by covering and packaging or by preservation such as freezing.

Vegetables lose water after they have been harvested, becoming shrivelled and limp

Foods also contain micro-organisms such as yeasts, moulds and bacteria which under the right conditions, especially in a warm temperature, will make foods go off.

In addition to water and micro-organisms foods also contain *enzymes*. These are chemicals naturally present in the cells of all foods. Enzymes speed up the chemical reactions of ripening and decay in foods and continue to work even after harvesting or slaughter. Enzymes are responsible for the ripening of fruits which is why a hard peach, pear or avocado will eventually soften and become ripe if stored in a dark place. If enzymes continue to work the food will eventually rot and decay.

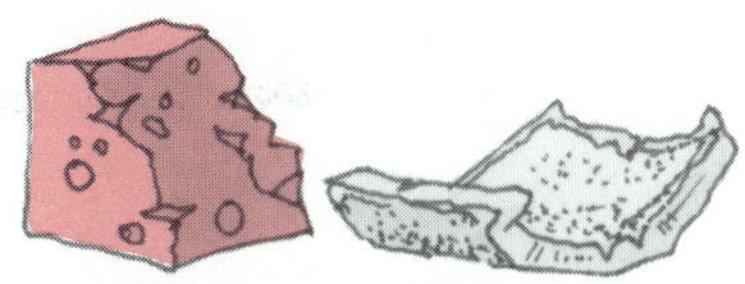

Cheese, meat, bread and fish will also lose water and dry out, especially if they are not covered

The enzymes and micro-organisms which destroy food are very sensitive to different temperatures.

To find out more about how temperature affects enzymes and micro-organisms look at the thermometer picture shown here.

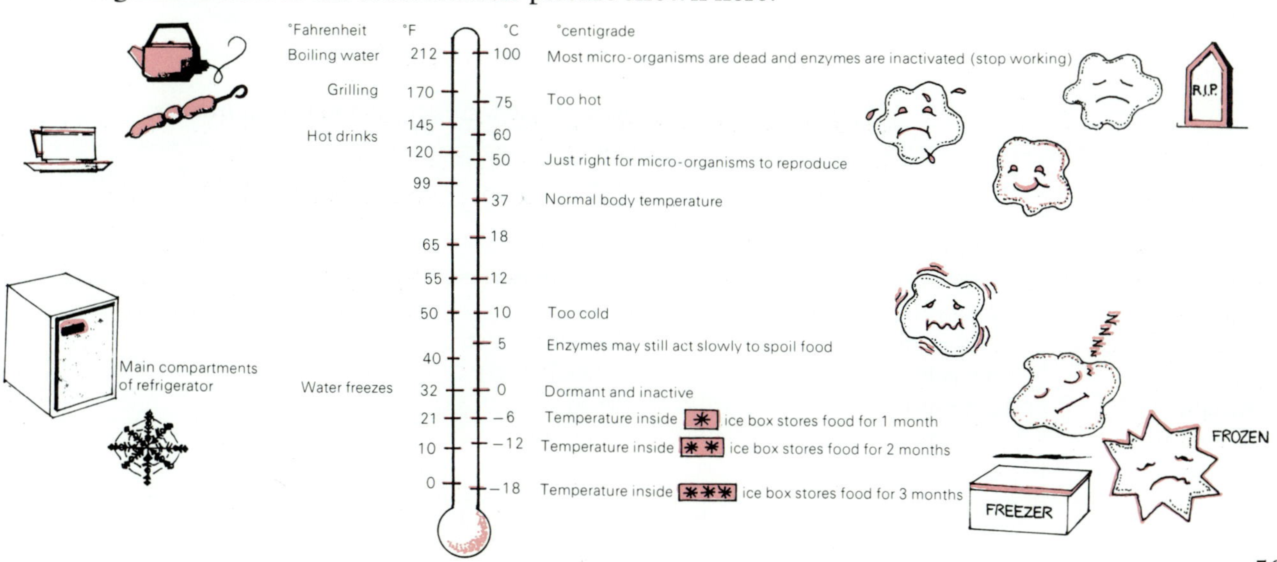

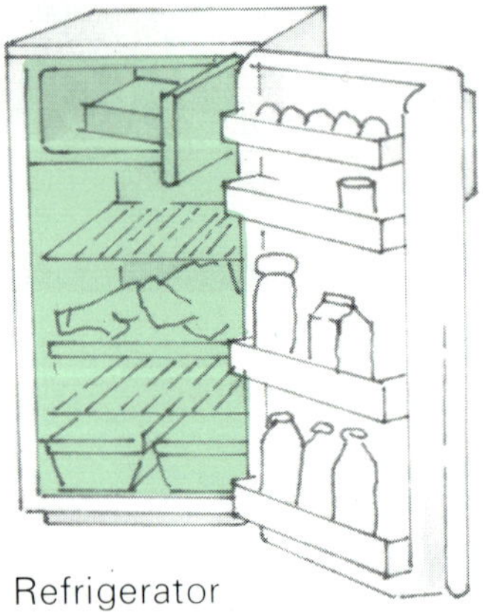

Refrigerator

It is possible to control the activity of micro-organisms and enzymes by using extremes of temperature. At very cold temperatures their activity is very slow or retarded and at freezing point will even stop. At boiling or near boiling temperatures enzymes and most micro-organisms are killed and will stop working.

A refrigerator and a freezer can both be used to control the storage temperature of foods so that they stay fresher for longer. Foods stored in this way must be covered to stop the surface of the food drying out because of water loss.

Frozen foods can be kept for up to three months depending on the star rating of the freezer compartment.

$-6°$ * up to 1 month
$-12°$ ** up to 2 months
$-18°$ *** up to 3 months

In the main compartment covered foods are kept clean and fresh.

Freezers

Freezers come in various shapes and sizes. Because the temperature inside a freezer is very low ($-18°C$) covered foods can be kept for quite a long time without spoiling. Foods do not keep forever in a freezer so it is important that you follow the storage instructions on packets and know the storage times for different foods.

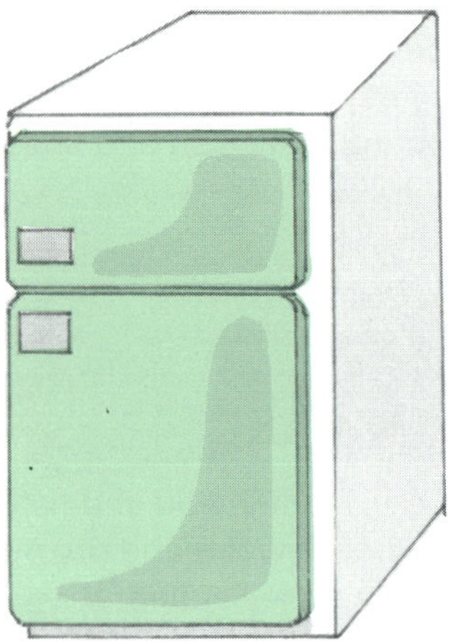

Fridge freezer

Upright freezer

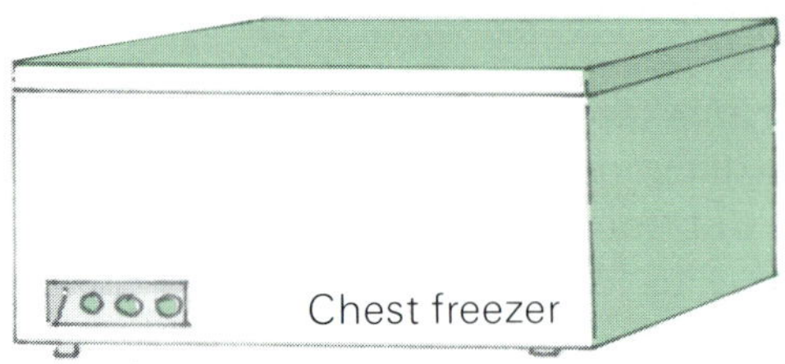

Chest freezer

Chart to show the storage time for various foods in a freezer.

Food	Keep in a freezer for up to	Food	Keep in a freezer for up to
Vegetables	12 months	Shell fish	2 months
Fruits	12 months	Hard cheese	3 months
Beef	12 months	Cakes	4 months
Minced beef	2 months	Uncooked pastry	3 months
Sausages	6 weeks	Cooked pastry	6 months
Chicken	12 months	Bread	3 months
White fish	8 months	Ice cream	3 months
Oily fish	4 months		

Freezing foods

Some foods can be carefully wrapped, labelled and put in a freezer straight away for storage. Commercially, frozen foods are packed ready for the freezer. Some foods such as fresh vegetables and fruits must be prepared before they are packed for freezing by *blanching*. Leafy green vegetables, peas, beans and root vegetables such as carrots and parsnips should be blanched to inactivate the enzymes. To blanch vegetables they must be plunged into boiling water for a few minutes and then plunged into very cold water, before they are drained and packed for freezing. Vegetables which have not been blanched will not keep for very long and their taste and colour will be affected.

Work in twos to carry out the following experiment.

Experiment to find out the effect of blanching on vegetables

You will need

200 grams prepared green leafy vegetables (brussels sprouts, cabbage)
1 large saucepan with a lid
1 large metal sieve or colander
1 large bowl half-full of water and a few ice cubes
2 freezer bags and ties
2 labels
1 slotted spoon
a watch, cooker timer or stop watch

Method

1 Half fill the saucepan with water and put over a medium heat to boil.
2 Weigh out 100 grams of vegetables and place them in a freezer bag. Exclude (press out) all the air and seal the bag with the tie. Label this bag as shown in the margin.
3 When the water in the saucepan is boiling (bubbling) gently lower in all the remaining vegetables using a slotted spoon.
4 Wait until the water boils again and then blanch the vegetables for only 3 to 4 minutes – time this carefully.
5 As soon as the time is up, carefully take the saucepan over to a sink and pour the vegetables into a colander to drain away the hot water.
6 Use a slotted spoon to place the vegetables in the icy cold water. This will quickly cool the vegetables and stop any further cooking.
7 When the vegetables are cold drain them well, shaking off any excess water. Then pack these vegetables into a freezer bag, exclude any air and tie firmly. Make a label as shown in the margin.

8 Put both bags into a deep freezer so that they are quickly frozen and leave for two to three weeks.
9 In your book draw a results chart like the one shown here.

Vegetables —cooked	*Smell*	*Colour and texture*	*Taste*
Blanched			
Unblanched			

To allow for the vegetables to be frozen for a length of time you will have to complete the next part of this experiment in another lesson.
10 After 2 to 3 weeks remove the vegetables from the freezer, thaw and then cook in salted boiling water. Drain the vegetables ready for tasting.
11 Look carefully at each of the cooked samples and discuss what you can see with the rest of the class and your teacher.
12 Taste each of the vegetable samples and then complete the results chart in your book.

You might like to try this next part at home

There is usually a star rating on packets of frozen foods to tell you how long to store them in the freezer or freezer compartment of a refrigerator.

Make a survey of frozen foods to find out their star rating and the recommended storage time.

Draw a chart like the one shown here to record your findings. An example has been started for you.

Frozen food	*Star rating*	*Storage time*	*Where the food should be stored (freezer etc.)*
Peas			

MONEY MANAGEMENT

Topic 17

In this topic you are going to think about how you use another resource – money.

The amount of money you get each week, your *weekly income*, can be spent in a variety of ways. How far your money stretches really depends on how you choose to spend it. It could be spent all at once on one or two items, spent in small amounts over several days or some of the money could be saved. To make the most of your weekly income you do need to plan exactly how it is going to be spent or saved.

Before you can begin to plan your spending you need to know exactly how much your weekly income is and where it comes from.

To find out your usual total income and expenditure draw a chart like the one shown here and fill it in. Special annual amounts of money, for example birthday or New Year money should not be included in this list. An example has been started for you.

Weekly income £.p	*From?*	*Weekly expenditure £.p*	*On?*
0.75	*Pocket money*	*0.27*	*Magazine*
0.70	*Car washing for friends, family*	*0.50*	*Entertainment*
		0.54	*Sweets*
0.40	*Collecting shopping for grandparent*	*0.65*	*Coca Cola*
	= Total weekly income		*= Total weekly expenditure*

Now work out how much of your total weekly income is spent by subtracting the total weekly expenditure from the total weekly income. For example:

	£.p.	
Total income	2.25	
Total expenditure	1.98	
	0.27	(+27p in credit)

Study the balance of your weekly income (the money left over).

If you spend *less than your income each week* then your balance will be *in credit* or *in the black.*

If you spend *more than your income each week* then your balance will be *overdrawn* or *in the red.*

If you found that you did spend more than your income write down in a sentence how much extra you spent and where this extra money came from.

Realizing exactly where your money goes

Draw either a histogram or a pie chart in your book, to show how much of the weekly income that you have just recorded is spent on different items.
For example:

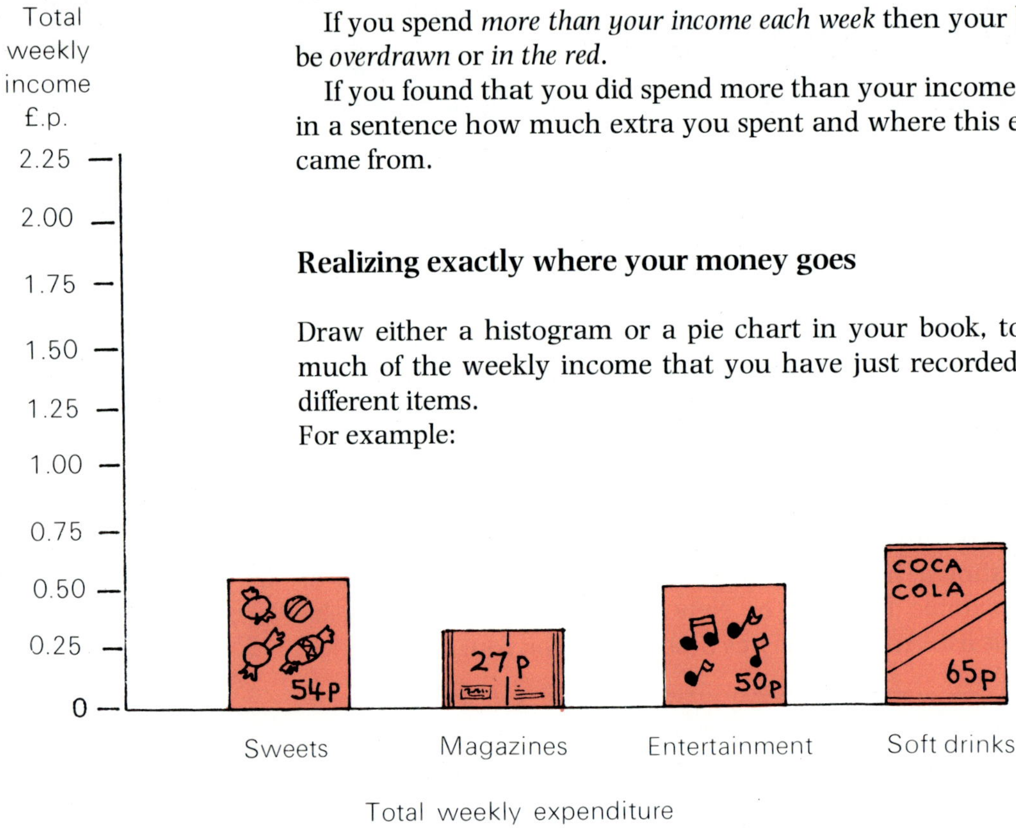

Find out your average income for a whole year by multiplying:

Your total weekly income £2.25p	×	52 (weeks in the year)	=	Yearly income

Now work out your average expenditure over a whole year.

Then in your book record this information in a chart like the one shown here. An example has been done for you.

	£. p.
Average yearly income	*117.00*
Average yearly expenditure	*102.96*
Balance	*14.04*

Apart from your average income there may also be special amounts of money that you get sometimes for example, birthday or holiday money. This extra money would be added to your total yearly income.

Write a sentence to say how you usually spend any extra money you get. Is it saved, spent straight away on small items, or spent on one larger item that you really needed or wanted?

Use a sentence to answer these questions in your book.

- Did you discover anything about your weekly or yearly income which surprised you?
- Were you surprised by how much or how little you spend each week and each year?
- Were you surprised by the total weekly amount you spent on any one item?
- If you wanted to spend less of your weekly income so that you could save more money, which items on your expenditure list would you spend less on?

Group 1

Can of coke

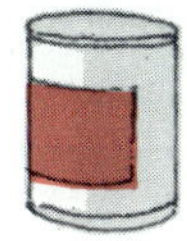

Price 28p
Size 500 ml

Bottle

Price 72p
Size $2\frac{1}{4}$ litres

Group 2

Crisps value pack

Crisps
Price 12p
Weight 25 grams

Crisps (large)
Price 45p
Size 150 grams

Price 62p
Size 6 packs
× 25 grams each

Group 3

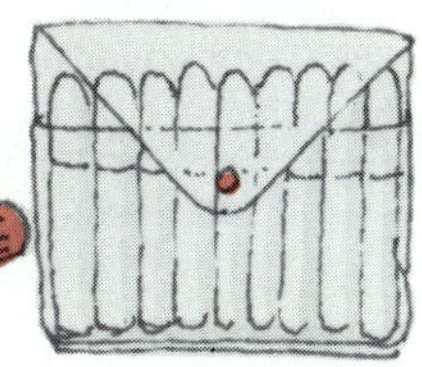

Single pen
Price 22p

Bumper value pack
Price 99p

How to get value for money

Several small amounts of items are usually more expensive than one large amount such as, a value pack. You could perhaps save money by making use of value packs so that you do not have to buy items every single day. Can you think of any other ways in which you could save money? Discuss your answer with your teacher and the rest of the class.

Look carefully at the groups of items shown in the margin and discuss what you can see with the rest of the class and your teacher.

Then draw a chart like the one below and fill it in to show which items from each of the groups you think are the best value for money.

Item list	*Price*	*Which I think is the best value for money*	*Reason*	*Which item in each group I would buy*	*Reason*

You might like to try this next part at home

Use the information in this topic to help you to keep an exact record of your total income and expenditure during the next week and work out the balance left over.

Topic 18

CONSUMER SENSE

A consumer or customer is a person who buys goods such as, clothing, food, furniture, stereo equipment or services such as repairs, plumbing work or decorating. These goods or services can be purchased from companies, a wide variety of shops, markets and mail order firms. If you buy goods and services then you are a consumer and you should know something about the consumer laws which exist to protect you.

It is very frustrating and annoying when you have saved hard to buy something only to discover later that the goods are faulty.

Has this ever happened to you?

With your teacher and the rest of the class discuss and describe an item that you have purchased and later found to be faulty. You might also like to discuss what you did about the faulty goods.

To prevent this happening to you again there are several things you should do before you part with your hard-saved money.

Firstly shop around to find out which shops offer not just the cheapest price but also the best value for money.

Inspect the goods for any damage and faults before you buy. Ask to have batteries checked. Always look in the box to check that all the parts are there and undamaged.

Is there a guarantee? If so to what does it entitle you? Ask about repairs and servicing. What about spare parts? Can you get a refund if it does not work when you get home?

When you make a purchase always keep the receipt in a safe place.

There are also certain things you should know before you part with your money.

When you buy anything you and the trader or seller are making a contract. If anything does go wrong then it is the trader and not the manufacturer who should deal with it. All goods including food and sale goods bought from a trader are covered by special rules. These special rules are written in the *Sale of Goods Act* and they tell you the trader's obligations and the customer's rights. This law has three major rules which the trader is obliged to abide by so that the customer is protected from faulty goods.

1

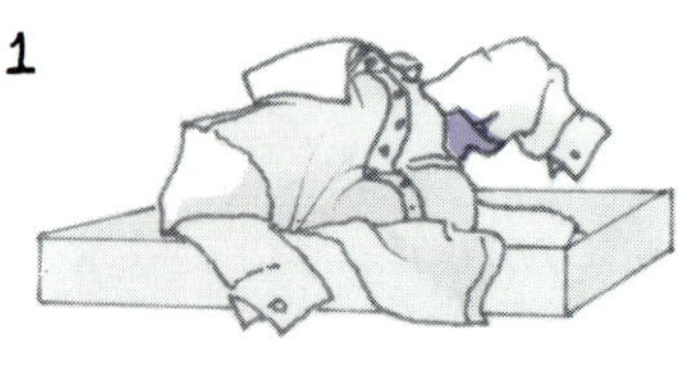

1 Any goods sold must be of merchantable quality and fit for their normal purpose. So new items must not be damaged, cracked or torn. However if goods are second-hand, marked as seconds or very cheap then you cannot expect top quality.

2 Goods should be as described on the label, package, display or by the trader. So shoes described as leather should not turn out to be plastic!
3 Goods must be fit for the purpose they are sold for. So an umbrella should not let the rain through.

2

3

If any of these rules is broken then customers are entitled to return the goods and can: ask for their money back; agree with the trader to an exchange or free repair.

The customer does not have to accept a credit note
Do not be put off by signs such as 'No refunds'. Such signs are illegal – even for sale goods. Traders cannot wriggle out of their obligations if they have sold you faulty goods.

Guarantees

Many goods have a guarantee. You should read and check this carefully as it may not cover everything, for example normal wear and tear. Whatever a guarantee says, if any one of the three rules is broken then you can still claim your rights from the trader.

However you are not entitled to anything if: you examined the item and should have seen the fault; you were told about the fault; you simply changed your mind about wanting the goods; you got the goods as a present (as only the buyer can make the claim).

Complaints

If you do have to make a complaint about faulty goods then you should: stop using the goods at once; tell the shop at once; take the goods back with the receipt or proof of purchase; ask for the manager or owner; be polite but firm and state your complaint clearly.

Getting help and advice

If you are not successful with your complaint then you can get free advice from your local *Consumer Advice Centre*. These centres are able to give advice on every aspect of buying and selling and so are useful to both trader and customer.

There are also local authority departments which can help you. The *Environmental Health Department* deals mainly with health matters such as, unfit food and drink, dirty restaurants and shops. The *Trading Standards* or *Consumer Protection Department* of your local authority will also be able to help you by: investigating misleading descriptions or prices; investigating inaccurate weights and measures; investigating the safety of goods; checking on the correct labelling of foods.

There may be a Citizens' Advice Bureau in your area which can also help with shopping complaints.

Work in small groups (two to four) to discuss one or two of the case studies shown here. Then use a sentence to answer the questions in your book. You can use the information given in this topic to help you. When all the groups have finished you might like to discuss each case study and the answers that you have given with the rest of the class and your teacher.

Case studies

Situation	Outcome	Questions
1 Saturday – person leaving shoe shop with new shoes.	That evening, out walking or dancing at disco. Heel comes off.	1 Which of the rules in the Sale of Goods Act has been broken? 2 What should the customer do next? 3 What is the trader obliged to do?
2 Man buying a shirt. He thinks it is about the right colour to match his suit so buys it.	He gets home. The shirt does not match. He decides to see if he can change it.	1 Which rule in the Sale of Goods Act has been broken? 2 Can the customer demand that the shirt be changed? 3 What is the trader obliged to do?
3 Boy takes 2-month old cassette radio back to shop as it is faulty. He takes along the receipt and guarantee too.	Trader says as there is a guarantee you have to write direct to the manufacturer.	1 Which rule in the Sale of Goods Act has been broken? 2 What are the customer's rights? 3 What is the trader obliged to do? 4 If this complaint fails what should the customer do?
4 Sales in electrical shop. Customer takes back a mixer. Says that mixer bought last week does not work. Asks for a refund.	Trader says – sorry but no refunds on sale goods, didn't customer see the sign?	1 Which rule in the Sale of Goods Act has been broken? 2 What are the customer's rights? 3 What is the trader obliged to do? 4 If the complaint fails what could the customer do?
5 Dress shop advertising pure silk dresses for sale at £20. Customer in the shop says the display says 'silk' but the label inside says 'cotton'. Asks for a refund.	Trader says – sorry we do not give cash refunds but customer can have a credit note.	1 Which rule in the Sale of Goods Act has been broken? 2 What are the customer's rights? 3 What is the trader obliged to do? 4 Does the customer have to accept a credit note?

You might like to try this next part at home

Find out the addresses of your nearest Consumer Advice Centre and Citizens' Advice Bureau and write them down in your book.

Topic 19

SMOKING

Being fit and healthy is something which is often taken for granted. People do not often appreciate good health until they are ill. Health can be affected by habits. For example: eating too much of the wrong foodstuffs like sugar and fat; eating too little of the right foodstuffs like dietary fibre; drinking too much alcohol; taking drugs; smoking.

All of these are things that each person has control over, or can make a decision about. So really ill health due to any of these reasons is avoidable and preventable. In this topic you are going to consider and discuss the facts about smoking and ill health.

Tobacco was discovered in America by Columbus in 1492 and the very first cigarette was probably invented in Spain during the 17th century. The habit of smoking grew and grew and now there are many millions of smokers who support a huge tobacco industry.

In twos look at the advertisements for cigarettes that your teacher has put on display. Then answer these questions in your book using a sentence.

- What are the people like who are shown in the advertisement? Are they young or old? Are they male or female?
- What are the people in the advertisement doing? Are they at work or relaxing?
- Perhaps there are no people in the advertisement – why do you think manufacturers use this style of advertising?
- Do all of the advertisements bear a government health warning?
- To whom do you think the advertisements are meant to appeal? Young people or older people? Men or women? People with lots or little money?
- Do you think cigarette packets should bear a government health warning?
- Do you think cigarettes should be advertised in magazines and on billboards?

You might like to discuss your answers with the rest of the class and the teacher.

What is a cigarette?
A cigarette is like a chemical factory which, when it is lit, produces more than 2000 known compounds many of which are poisonous. The most dangerous compounds found in a cigarette are, tar, nicotine and carbon monoxide.

Carbon monoxide, is a colourless gas found in tobacco smoke. This chemical seriously reduces the oxygen carrying capacity of red blood cells and this means that the body gets less oxygen than it really needs. To compensate for the lack of oxygen the heart and lungs have to work much harder and are put under great strain.

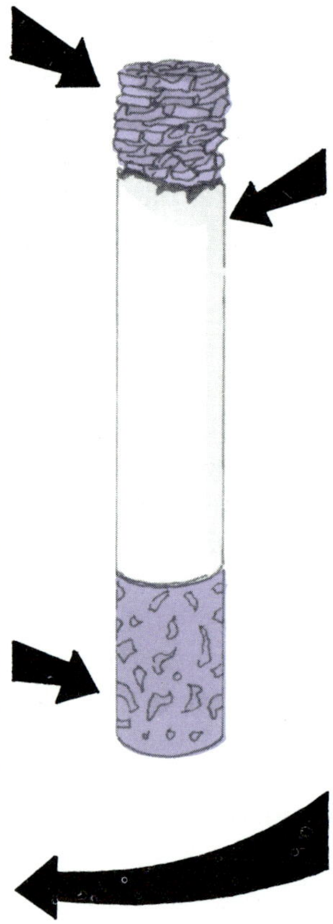

Nicotine, is a powerful poison found in cigarettes and it is very addictive. A single drop of nicotine (about 70 milligrams) injected into the bloodstream could kill a person. Nicotine has a serious effect on the brain cells and causes the craving for more. With each cigarette, smokers take in about 1 milligram of nicotine.

Tar – liquid tobacco tar is produced from a burning cigarette. This tar coats the airways of the lungs and makes breathing difficult. The tar damages the lungs and is known to cause cancer.

There have been many reports published by doctors about the harmful effects of smoking. Each year thousands of pounds are spent on health education campaigns telling people to stop smoking. Cigarette advertising on television has been banned since 1965 however many advertisements do appear in magazines and on billboards. Every packet of cigarettes must bear a government health warning.

What smoking does to the body
In order to live we all need to breathe oxygen. The parts of the body involved in breathing are the trachea (windpipe), bronchi, lungs and air sacs and the diaphragm.

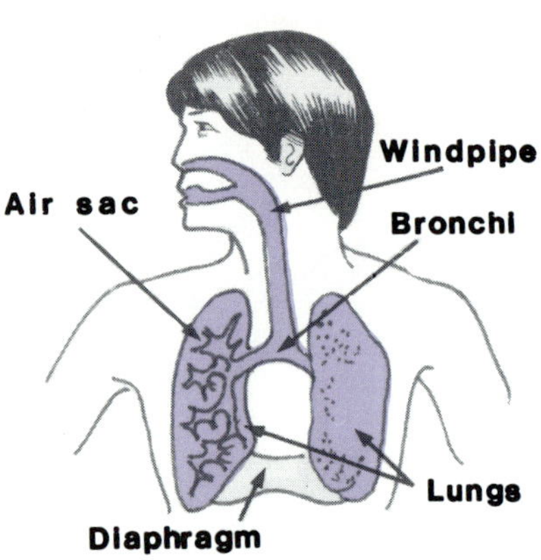

When a cigarette is smoked tar, nicotine and carbon monoxide are sucked down into the delicate tubes of the lungs where they cause irritation.

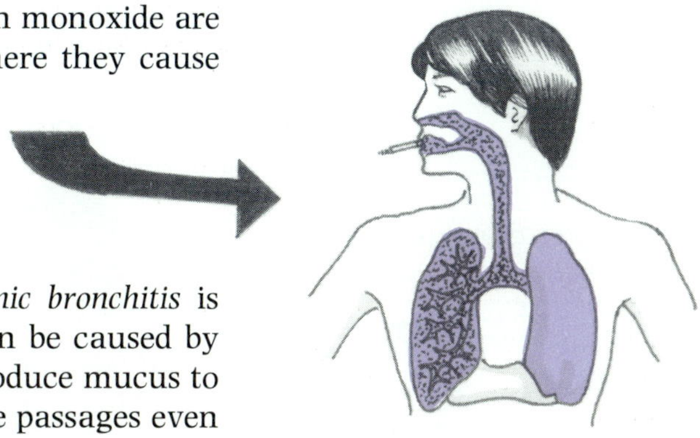

Bronchitis is inflammation of the air passages. *Chronic bronchitis* is inflammation which lasts for a long time and this can be caused by smoking. When the air passages are inflamed they produce mucus to soothe the irritation and this extra mucus clogs up the passages even more. To clear the passages the person smoking has to cough – sometimes called the 'smoker's cough'. Chronic bronchitis is a serious disease which causes a lot of suffering.

Lung cancer is a serious disease known to be caused by smoking. Cancer in the lungs prevents them from working properly. Lung cancer can take up to 20 years to develop and it is more likely to happen to a smoker than to a non-smoker. Not every person who smokes gets lung cancer but for every ten people who die from lung cancer nine are smokers.

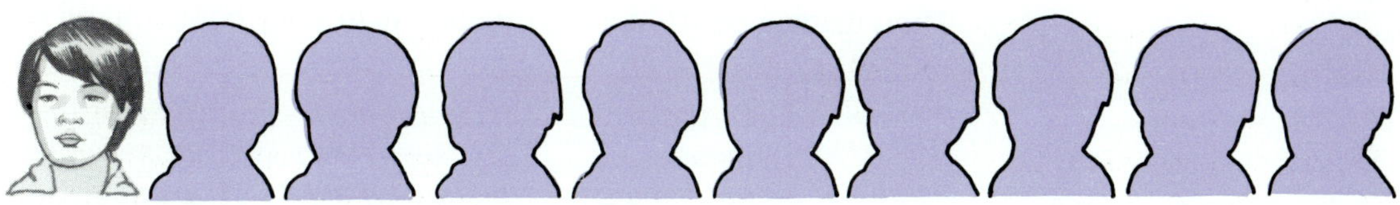

Smoking is especially dangerous for pregnant women. Smoking affects the growth of the unborn baby and women who do smoke in pregnancy are more likely to have premature or underweight babies.

Hot cigarette smoke also damages the taste buds on the tongue and the cells responsible for smelling in the nose. So a smoker's senses of smell and taste are also affected.

The nicotine in cigarettes also causes yellowing of the teeth and fingers. The smoke from cigarettes makes breath, hair, clothes and rooms smell.

Who else is affected by smoking?

When people who do not smoke are affected by cigarette smoke from people who do, this is known as passive smoking. Even breathing in someone else's cigarette smoke can be dangerous and if this goes on for a long time, perhaps through living in the same house as a smoker or working in a room with smokers, it can cause serious illness for non-smokers as well as being unpleasant.

In twos look at the pictures shown here.

A

B

C

Then draw a chart like the one below in your book and fill it in.

Picture	*Describe what is happening*	*If I was the smoker in the picture what I would do*	*If I was the non-smoker in the picture what I would do*
A			
B			
C			

You might like to discuss your answers with the rest of the class and the teacher.

Consider these facts

Cigarette smoking increases the risk of lung cancer which kills over 38 000 people in the United Kingdom each year or 1 person every 14 minutes.

Chronic bronchitis which kills 24 000 people a year is much more likely to affect smokers.

Of every 1000 young people who smoke, 6 will be killed in traffic accidents but 250 will be killed by smoking.

On average a smoker shortens his or her life by $5\frac{1}{2}$ minutes for each cigarette smoked.

Infants under one year are twice as likely to develop a serious chest illness if both parents smoke.

Stillbirths (death at birth) and death in the first few weeks of life are increased by nearly one-third in smoking mothers compared to non-smoking mothers.

Imagine this situation

You and your best friend belong to a sports team. Your friend has started to smoke recently. You are concerned that his/her health might suffer and also that he/she might lose his/her place on the team.

In a paragraph write down what you might say to make him/her give up smoking.

Consider these facts

Between 1972 and 1978 cigarette smoking dropped among men from 52% to 45% and among women from 41% to 37%

About 2 million French people stopped smoking in the period 1975 to 1980.

75% of the world's airlines now provide non-smoking accommodation in their planes.

More and more restaurants, buses, trains, theatres and cinemas ban smoking or ask smokers to sit in special seats.

In recent years more and more people have given up smoking. Here is a list of some of the reasons why people do stop smoking. Work in small groups of up to four people to discuss which statements you think are most likely to be the reasons why people stop smoking. When your group has reached an agreement on the importance of each statement, rewrite the list in your book so that the reason which you thought would be most important is at the top and so on.

Smoking makes me cough
My teeth are yellow
I get out of breath easily
Smoking is an expensive habit
Other people wanted me to give up
There are 'no smoking' signs everywhere you go
My friends do not smoke
These days you are the odd one out if you do smoke
My breath smelt and so did my clothes

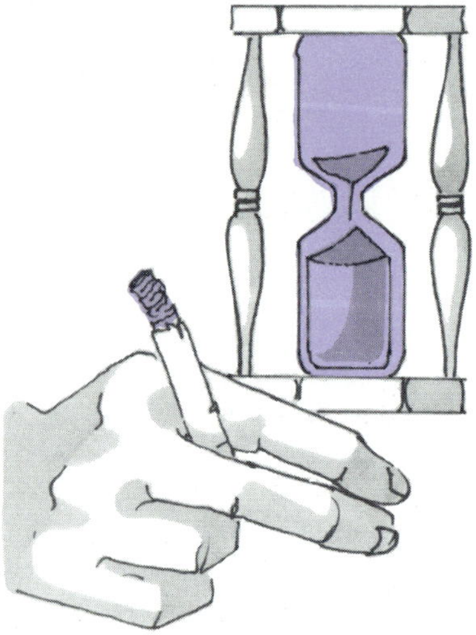

You might like to discuss your list with the rest of the class and the teacher.

In groups of two consider each of these statements. Then draw a table like the one shown below and fill it in to say whether you agree or disagree and why.

Children whose parents smoke are more likely to form the habit
Young people tend to copy the smoking habits of personalities they admire
Children start to smoke from curiosity and from the urge to experiment
Children consider smoking as a symbol of maturity
Classroom smokers are often below average at lessons and games
Children start smoking to be part of the crowd
Prospects of ill health or death are too remote to influence children
Children do not think it will become a real habit for them

Statement	*I agree* ✓	*I disagree* ✓	*Reason*

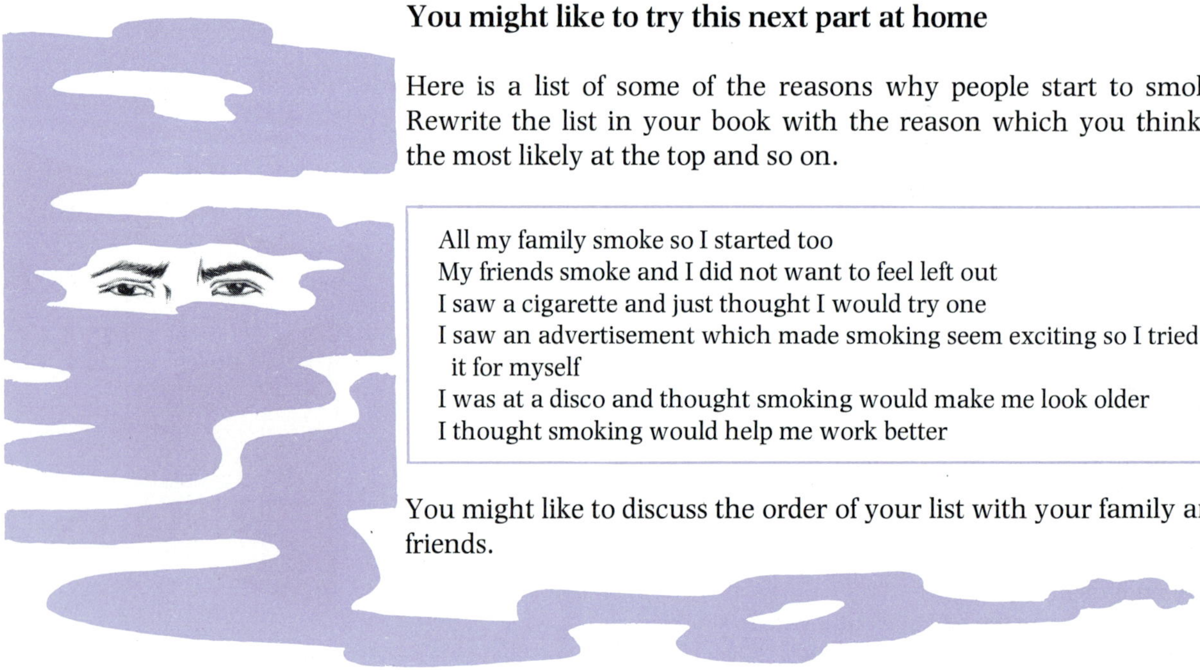

You might like to try this next part at home

Here is a list of some of the reasons why people start to smoke. Rewrite the list in your book with the reason which you think is the most likely at the top and so on.

All my family smoke so I started too
My friends smoke and I did not want to feel left out
I saw a cigarette and just thought I would try one
I saw an advertisement which made smoking seem exciting so I tried it for myself
I was at a disco and thought smoking would make me look older
I thought smoking would help me work better

You might like to discuss the order of your list with your family and friends.

DRUG ABUSE

Topic 20

Drugs have been used for hundreds and hundreds of years to cure illness and to relieve pain. A drug is any substance that acts on the central nervous system. Most drugs are poisons and for them to benefit the body they must be prescribed in safe amounts by a doctor who understands how they act in the body. Taken in the right quantities drugs can cure disease but any drug taken in the wrong amounts can cause death. All drugs prescribed or sold over the counter in chemists have strict dosage instructions on the label.

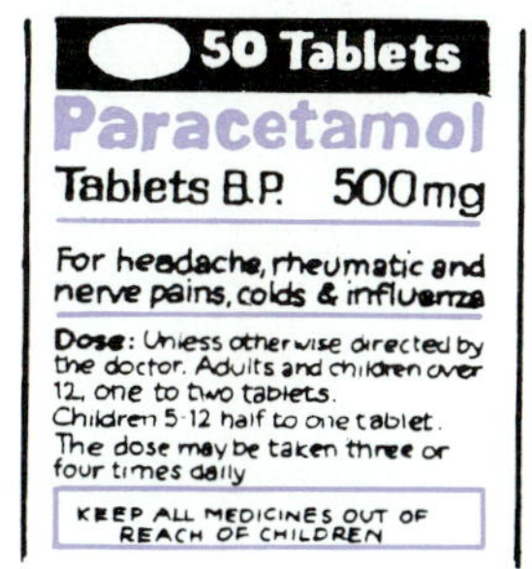

Questions	*My answer*	*My partner's answer*
Have you ever been prescribed drugs when you have been ill?		
In what form was the drug taken? Liquid, powder or tablet form?		
Can you remember the dose that you had to take?		
Have you noticed the safety warning on the labels of over-the-counter drugs?		
What type of safety warning is usually given?		
Do you ever take over-the-counter drugs. What for?		
Do you think they help to relieve the symptoms of your ailment?		
Where should drugs be kept for safety?		

Drugs which are sold over the counter such as, aspirin and cold remedies do not have to be prescribed by a doctor. However it is still necessary for people taking these drugs regularly to ask the advice of their doctor and to follow the dosage instructions carefully. Many over-the-counter drugs are not really needed as many illnesses especially headaches and colds will get better through time without the help of drugs. The problem is that people now expect instant relief from minor ailments. Also advertisements on the television and in magazines encourage people to take aspirins or cold remedies.

There are other non-prescribed drugs that people might take. Alcohol is a drug which is contained in many types of spirits, wines and beers. Alcohol also has an effect on the central nervous system and causes changes in mood and slows down the actions of the brain. Alcohol is called a depressant drug because it affects people's emotions and feelings. Even very small amounts of alcohol have an effect on the body and can be dangerous especially if someone tries to drive or work machinery after drinking. People can also become addicted to alcohol so that they come to depend on it and crave it more and more. Alcohol abuse causes serious damage to the body especially to the liver, kidneys and brain. Dependence on alcohol can also lead to social problems and people who drink a lot may lose their job, their family and friends. Alcohol is a legal drug but there are laws governing the sale of alcohol to people under 18 years.

Different alcoholic drinks contain different amounts of alcohol. As a rough guide:

$\frac{1}{2}$ pint of beer contains the same amount of alcohol as

1 glass of wine

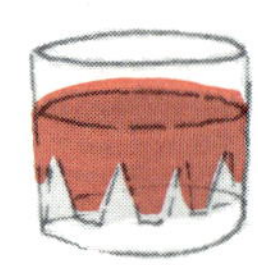

1 single whisky

Although it tastes sweet, cider is often actually stronger than many beers and will have an even greater effect on the body.

In twos look at the five pictures shown below and at the top of page 77. Then write one or two sentences in your book to describe what you think might be happening in each picture.

1

2

3

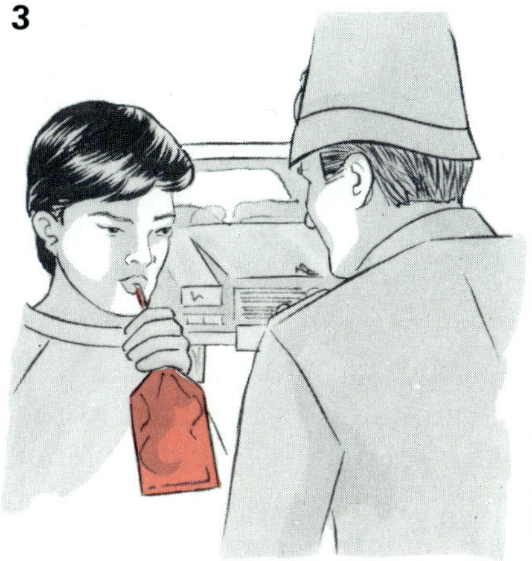

4

5

Illegal drugs

There are other drugs which are illegal. These drugs all have a very serious effect on the body and are also addictive. Having possession of illegal drugs or trying to sell them is a criminal offence.

Once addicted to a drug the user becomes dependent and craves more and more. It is also hard to stop taking drugs or to kick the habit because most of these drugs have withdrawal symptoms which cause physical pain. Drugs which are illegal are very expensive to buy and drug users are caught in a trap of having to find more and more money to support their habit. When drug users cannot afford the drugs that their bodies crave they may turn to crime, for example stealing or prostitution, to get money for drugs. Illegal drugs have a serious effect on the user's body and can bring about an early death. Drug-taking is also a secret business and users often become isolated from their families and friends. The life of a drug-user becomes centred on one thing – getting money to pay for their expensive habit.

Here are some of the reasons why young people may start to take illegal drugs. Work in pairs or threes to discuss and agree upon which statements are the most likely reasons why young people may start to take drugs. Then rewrite the list in your books in your agreed order of priority so that the most likely reason is at the top and so on.

The drugs are available
Drug taking is exciting
They think drug taking might help solve their problems
Their friends take drugs and they do not want to be left out
Drugs are offered to them to try
They want to experiment to find out what the drug will do to them

At the end of this task join the rest of your class and your teacher to discuss the order of your group's list.

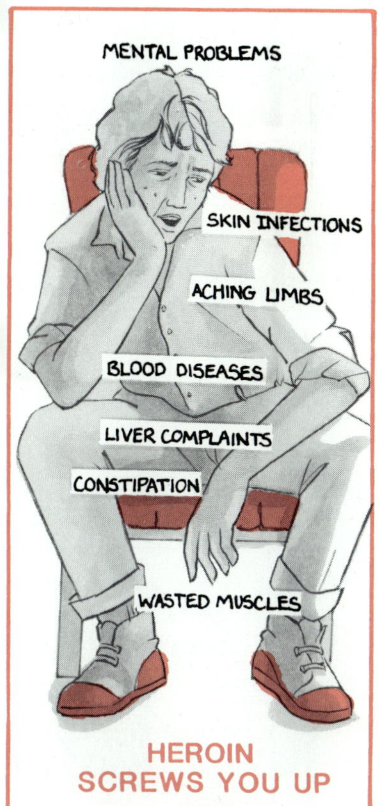

Adapted from an anti-heroin poster, published by the DHSS

Solvent abuse

Solvent abuse or 'glue sniffing' as it is sometimes called has become common among young people in recent years. In actual fact it is the vapour from the glue and not the glue or solvent itself that is sniffed or inhaled. Sniffing the vapour from solvents such as lighter fuel, adhesives or antifreeze has very serious effects on the body. The immediate effect of sniffing produces spots or rings around the nose and mouth, affects vision and hearing and causes mental confusion. Suffocation or fatal effects on the heart muscles have resulted in the death of some young people who have experimented with solvent abuse. If the sniffing habit goes on for a long time then physical damage to the kidneys, liver and nasal passages may even occur.

Consider these facts

More boys than girls from 11 to 16 years old misuse solvents.

At the present time it is not a criminal offence to misuse solvents.

Solvent abusers run the risk of serious injury or death.

People who use solvents often feel sick, suffer severe headaches, feel depressed and irritable.

Evidence suggests that heavy misuse of solvents can lead to dependence.

Sniffing usually takes place in secret among small groups of people.

People who do misuse solvents may go on to other drugs.

Solvent abuse causes drunken-like behaviour and affects the user's actions, speech and work.

Solvents are not hard to get hold of.

In groups of two write out a list in your book of reasons why you think young people may start glue sniffing. When you have finished discuss the list you have made with the rest of the class and the teacher.

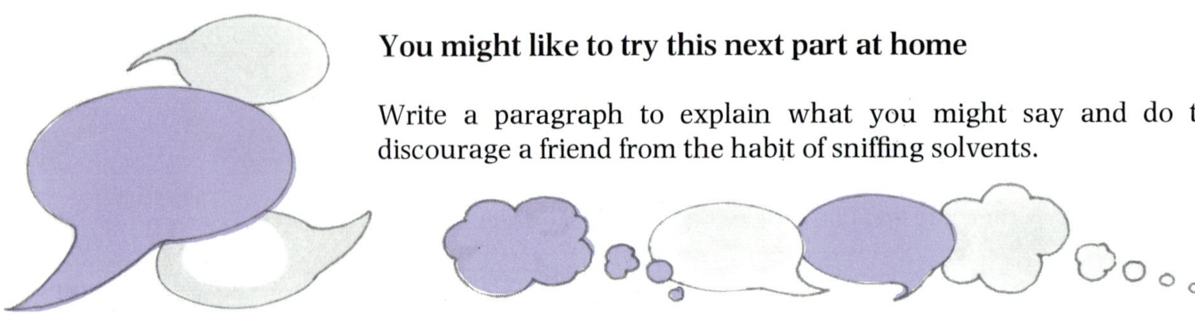

You might like to try this next part at home

Write a paragraph to explain what you might say and do to discourage a friend from the habit of sniffing solvents.